The End of the Tito Era

The End of the Tito Era

Yugoslavia's Dilemmas

Slobodan Stanković

HOOVER INSTITUTION PRESS

Stanford University   Stanford, California

*The Hoover Institution on War, Revolution and Peace, founded at
Stanford University in 1919 by the late President Herbert Hoover,
is an interdisciplinary research center for advanced study on
domestic and international affairs in the twentieth century. The views
expressed in its publications are entirely those of the authors
and do not necessarily reflect the views of the staff, officers,
or Board of Overseers of the Hoover Institution.*

Hoover Press Publication 236

Designed by Elizabeth Gehman

In memory of my late brother, Vojislav

Contents

~~~~~~
Editor's Foreword

If one could express in a single statement the source of uncertainty that in so many minds accompanies the passing of the Tito era, it might refer to the dangers of excessive political longevity. After the Communists seized political power in Yugoslavia during the fall of 1944, Josip Broz Tito (secretary general of the movement since 1937) had the decisive voice in devising the main political line. He maneuvered and, when necessary, imposed his will on various factions within the party; elaborated and, with extraordinary single-mindedness, shaped the country's foreign affairs—in brief, surrounded his policies not only with an extraordinary "cult of personality," but constructed a political system that became nearly his own exclusive domain of action on domestic as well as on international levels.

And yet Tito represented neither a totalitarian leader before his conflict with Stalin in 1948, nor a conventional authoritarian despot after that event. He was never interested in political theory per se, beyond the elementary need for his system to have a legitimizing doctrine as do other Marxist party-ruled states. An extraordinary propensity for personal luxury, which blended rather curiously with the deep and everlasting communist convictions of his youth, the Comintern days, and the "people's liberation struggle" during World War II, imparted to the system of socialist self-management and socialist market economy (the two basic tenets of Titoism) a measure of leniency as long as citizens did not question the party's monopoly in the political sphere.

The basic problem, so well covered in the author's lucid study, involves the fact that Tito presided over the emergence of an extremely complex socioeconomic system and yet failed to clarify its very essence. As already suggested, he skillfully maneuvered among groups and individuals who had different views about solutions for the country's problems. Instead of attempting to solve those problems in a coherent and decisive manner, Tito remained at "dead center" and resolutely eliminated political opponents but did not encourage genuine reform.

It was typical of his long reign that on countless occasions Tito criticized weaknesses in the economy and preached the absolute necessity for "stabilization." And yet for years, the latter has remained the most elusive aspect of economic performance. Fully aware of the basic contradiction in the system, namely irreconcilability between the principle of self-management and the dominant rule of the communist party, he did nothing. Tito had left to his closest comrade-in-arms, the late Edvard Kardelj, the indispensable and potentially dangerous task of extolling in endless theoretical variations the virtues of "pluralism of self-management," the very word "pluralism" being unacceptable to the party faithful. How, indeed, could the requirements of socioeconomic "pluralism" and the officially recognized necessity of maintaining "democratic centralism" within the League of Communists become reconciled?

Facing this dilemma, especially since 1974 when he forcefully proclaimed that "liberalism" was not to be tolerated, Tito candidly expressed his progressive loss of faith in the party's ability to maintain the achievements of his regime. In contrast, he increasingly insisted that the purest element of Titoist orthodoxy resided in the armed forces, the only "genuine" Yugoslav body, unspoiled by the party's proclivity to split along republican lines and defend local interests. The growing number of generals heading civilian institutions marks another strange feature of Tito's military predilections. As the author argues, the army could pursue its military duties effectively but would be the least competent body to administer and find solutions to economic problems that confound the best minds among Yugoslav politicians and economists.

One remains skeptical that the problem of succession, so carefully devised, will work at both state and party levels. The main function of these short-term rotating systems is to eliminate any temptation to install longer lasting "leaders." The longest lasting leader at the end of his life had thundered against any individual who would exercise power as he did. More important is that nothing in the political history of Yugoslavia during the past 35 years suggests that a "Swiss" formula of collective leadership and personal anonymity at the top could work in a country that had known so many crises since the party came to power. More important, nonviolent solutions to these crises had required a supreme arbiter (Tito) to whose will everybody appeared ready to bow. The fact that nobody within the movement even begins to approach Tito's authority begs the question whether collective leaderships are appropriate tools for solving difficult and in some instances even organic problems. Assuming a priori that the problem of Tito's succession cannot be solved would be a mistake, but the ostentatious optimism of Yugoslav officialdom on this score should leave any observer with a solid dose of skepticism.

And then there remains for Yugoslavia the question of how the USSR will react to Tito's succession. One certainly should exclude, at least for the immediate future, any Afghanistan-type, direct Soviet army intervention. On the other hand, as the author suggests, Yugoslavia's internal contradictions (especially those of a multiple ethnic nature) offer to Kremlin leaders possibilities for destabilization of a post-Tito regime. Tito's successors easily might be forced to seek accommodation with the USSR at the expense of a traditional balancing formula. On the other hand, relations with the Soviets could worsen, providing Moscow with other tools of pressure, including the "Brezhnev doctrine." Still, and here an imaginative and firm policy in the West could stop Kremlin temptations, one could imagine and hope for a post-Tito political evolution, based on solid evidence that the overwhelming majority of Yugoslavia's citizens reject in their everyday behavior any inclination to become once again part of the Soviet-directed "commonwealth of nations."

The author has offered so much hard information and sober analysis that this book represents a first-rate contribution toward a better understanding of the most complicated country in East-Central Europe and the Balkans.

RICHARD F. STAAR

Director of International Studies
Hoover Institution

Preface

As the Tito era in Yugoslavia came to an end, serious problems confronted the nation. Tito's longevity and his prestige had allowed Yugoslavs to ignore these problems or to pretend that they had been overcome. Chief among these is the question of the succession, an often apparently solved problem that bedeviled Yugoslavs during the long years of Tito's incumbency. Other major problems are the economic situation, the fate of the late Edvard Kardelj's concept of the "pluralism of self-management interests," Soviet-Yugoslav relations, and the role of Yugoslavia's army after Tito's disappearance from the political scene.

These are not the only problems that Yugoslavia faces, but given the limited space available, it was impossible to consider at length such issues as the electoral system, the persecution of dissidents, or Yugoslav-American and Yugoslav-Chinese relations. These issues are therefore mentioned only in passing in the concluding chapter.

In discussing Yugoslav theories, I am in every case referring to official theories rather than those, for example, of such critics of the system as the contributors to the Zagreb philosophical bimonthly *Praxis*, which was banned in 1975. It should be emphasized, however, that certain "official" theories are not necessarily official, although publicized by the Yugoslav media. In this regard, official approval is often tacit. Conversely, Kardelj's theories, which were the basis for the June 1978 congress of the League of Communists of Yugoslavia, can no longer necessarily be considered the party's official line. Since Kardelj's death in February 1979, Yugoslavia's leaders and major theorists have ceased mentioning them. In addition, much of the terminology current in Yugoslavia is vague, in many cases intentionally so. It cannot, therefore, always be taken at face value. This is true even of such well-known terms as "self-management system."

The appendix contains biographies of the 30 most important political personalities in Yugoslavia, in addition to President Tito's, who died on 4 May 1980, only a few days before his 88th birthday. It is from among these 30 top leaders that Tito's successor or successors will probably be found.

I should like to thank Radio Free Europe, under whose auspices much of the original research for this book was done and whose encouragement enabled me to complete it.

ONE

Tito and
the Yugoslav Dilemma

With President Tito's death on 4 May 1980 an era in the life of communist Yugoslavia came to an end. Although almost 88 years old, President Josip Broz Tito had until the end of 1979 almost complete control both of the Socialist Federative Republic of Yugoslavia (SFRY) and of the League of Communists of Yugoslavia (LCY).[1] This had both positive and negative aspects. Positively, President Tito's longevity had undeniably preserved the country's (and party's) unity, without which Yugoslavia could not exist. On the other hand, it made a smooth transition from his rule virtually impossible. Despite all the claims made during the long process of Tito's death that everything had been going smoothly, the attempts made to ensure an orderly succession were more theoretical than practical. The weaknesses in Yugoslav society will become apparent only after a certain time has elapsed after his death, for only his unchallenged authority had prevented sharp internal confrontation. Just as after Stalin's death in the Soviet Union and Mao's death in China, in Yugoslavia, too, it will very soon become clear that the "great leader" has left behind him not only firm postulates for a strong state and a united party, but also much confusion in all spheres of the country's and party's life. Much of the confusion was visible already during his lifetime, but much more was concealed by Tito's great authority when he resolved serious problems either by a "letter" to party members or by introducing purges. These kinds of solutions will no longer be possible.

In the past three decades, Tito and his followers rejected as outdated many of Marx's, Engels's, and Lenin's theories and instead "creatively developed" many new ones. Two of these have played a major role in Yugoslavia's development: the withering away of the state and the withering away of the party. The emphasis has changed from period to period, but the principal argument has remained the same: permanent internal conflicts have characterized not only the noncommunist (capitalist) systems but also the communist-ruled countries. Conflicts in the latter are camouflaged, however, by the alleged harmony of various interests.

Not everything said or written in Yugoslavia about this subject should be regarded as a developed vision of the future. Rather, official Yugoslav theories about the party's withering away consist of various specialized and often deliberately unclear theses that share only a reaction to the inevitable changes wrought by reality. In examining the numerous official theories, therefore, we should not assume that everything Yugoslav theorists advocate has been implemented. Whatever theories party leaders have held, they have never been willing to relinquish their monopoly of power. At the same time, however, they have always been aware (the late Edvard Kardelj was the most articulate on this point) that one-party dictatorship, especially the form prevailing in Eastern Europe, cannot survive without greater freedom both for theorists and for the population as a whole. The dilemma confronting the LCY is that this cannot be achieved without reorganizing the party from within, and without depriving the party of its monopoly to make decisions about questions vitally important both to the people and the state.

Since 1950 Yugoslav theorists have attempted to create a society in which the dictatorship of the proletariat would become what Rosa Luxemburg in her interpretation of Marx had advocated—namely, a society that is the achievement of the working class and working people. In this society workers would control all institutions performing protective functions (such as the police and the army). If the Yugoslav answer to this problem, the self-management system proclaimed in 1950, were to become a reality, however, then actual democracy for the masses would exist only if they participated in the management of the economy, as well as of state, political, and other public affairs, on a day-to-day basis. This, however, has not occurred.

At this juncture two questions about the role of the party arose. Should the party really wither away? If it did, who would then "teach" the masses? After Milovan Djilas's purge in 1954, Tito, Kardelj, and their followers continued to emphasize the general value of the self-management system but firmly insisted that the party should not wither away. Rather its essence should be changed. Its role, they claimed, was defined in the *Communist Manifesto*, which stated that a communist party should have no special interests of its own vis-à-vis the working class as a whole. The success of a party depends on its leaders' understanding of the reality in which they live, on the natural links of the party with the proletariat, and finally, on its organizational forms, which must be altered according to the conditions under which the party operates. Some of these ideas are included in the party program adopted at the Seventh LCY Congress in April 1958, a program that is still officially valid, although in many ways abrogated by subsequent changes.

Official Yugoslav party theorists, such as the Croat Vladimir Goati, have tried to describe "truthfully the contradictory reality of socialist societies." They have emphasized one essential fact: in socialist societies there are various group interests that "are neither remnants of the old [capitalist] society nor the result of foreign influences, but actually legitimate products of socialist development."[2] Another theorist, Velizar Šerer, admitted that in Yugoslavia, too, "there have been problems with the formation of groups, informal cliques, and factions not only in the system of associated labor [enterprises] but also outside it, a problem that has not been subjected to any scientific research."[3] Instead of workers, managing their own factories, "various power centers" still make decisions in the workers' name without consulting them, according to Šerer. In his opinion, "the workers' insufficiently developed consciousness" has made them "passive observers" on whom those at the top have easily imposed everything they wanted.

This situation could lead only to instability, which is, according to Kardelj, "a source of nondemocratic practices." He believed that only stability, achieved by securing the leading role of a definite (working) class in power by having its representatives hold key positions, allows democracy to develop. Yugoslav leaders appear to want both a highly developed "democratic self-management system," with the public free to make its own decisions without commands from above, and a strictly disciplined party preventing the masses from straying or opposing party interests. These leaders obviously fear the fundamental contradiction in the Titoist system, which Milovan Djilas pointed out in 1953: any attempt to achieve genuine liberalization in a one-party dictatorship must release forces that, in the end, will conflict with the one-party system. Djilas, in his article "An Answer," said: "We have entered the epoch of struggle for democracy, and neither will we nor can we withdraw from it. This struggle can be slowed down, delayed, but not halted."[4]

Party officials in the post-Djilas era have tried to resolve the dilemma between development of a democratically based self-management system and full control by an authoritarian party apparatus representing a tiny minority within the country. Kardelj, in his last book, explained this complex duality:

> We do not favor minority rule, even though the League of Communists represents a minority and has to be a minority because only as such, in our case, can it act as the vanguard of social progress and only as such can it review socialist practice as a whole. But the party should not impose a monopolistic rule over society . . . The party must employ democratic methods of action.[5]

Party leaders have found this a difficult concept to implement, however. The very leaders who vociferously demand "democratic methods of action" encourage the existence of "hierarchical relations" at all levels. "People who feel powerful in 'their own house' have to an increasing extent attempted to strengthen their position by joining forces with similar party officials elsewhere. This in fact leads to the formation of informal cliques composed of 'champions' who frequently hold virtually all the decision-making strings in their own hands."[6] This frank and courageous admission by the Belgrade writer Slobodan Vujica came during polemics over the methods needed to strengthen collective responsibility in all aspects of Yugoslav society—that is, the way in which Tito's idea of collective leadership should be implemented.

Vujica revealed that disputes between "professional officials" and "nonprofessional members of various forums" had created extensive problems. "Is it realistic to expect the apparatus of a political forum or a managerial board to treat a nonprofessional member of such an agency and a professional member of the same forum, the latter being at the same time the former's immediate boss, in the same way? Recent discussions have frequently raised this question." Vujica concluded that this expectation was unreasonable, adding that "nonprofessional members of forums have frequently been made to feel like 'guests' who have aroused consternation among the professional apparatus by insisting too much on or demanding too stubbornly something beyond the prescribed and strictly limited work of the forum."[7] Therefore, in Yugoslavia it is easy to denounce both those who obey and those who disobey laws and regulations as saboteurs of the system.

Professor Andrija Krěsić explains this dilemma in Yugoslavia's self-management socialism as the party's reaction to domestic and foreign conditions "now in the direction of a political one-party dictatorship and now in the direction of a special sort of plebeian ultra-democratism." He claims that this oscillation "can sometimes be noted in two successive speeches by one and the same political leader." Since pronouncements about the programmatic character of the self-management system and its "strategic visions" are easier to express than to practice, "the authors of the pronouncements come into conflict with members of the same party when the latter attempt to comply with the proclaimed declarations faithfully."[8] Hence, so-called classical political rule and the new direct, self-managing democracy inevitably contradict one another; each restricts the other and neither realizes its full potential as originally conceived. Consequently they disappoint both those making the pronouncements and those in charge of implementing them.

This tension has not promoted unity in the country and the party. Rather it has determined that under the same communist symbols different political ideas exist, in many cases colored with more or less extreme nationalistic views. The credit for preventing these political differences from openly conflicting must again be given to President Tito and his unchallenged authority. But whither Yugoslavia after him? The task of this book is to give at least a partial answer to this question.

TWO

The Vicious Circle in the Economic System

The economic situation in Yugoslavia has seldom been totally satisfactory, but a particularly negative trend set in during the early 1970s. Various external and internal pressures produced a number of serious difficulties not solvable by accepted economic measures. Moreover, the improvements expected from the radical economic reforms of 1965 failed to materialize. These reforms were a desperate attempt by Yugoslav leaders to initiate what they believed to be a fruitful combination of the Western market economy and socialist centralized planning as practiced in the East—in both cases, of course, in a revised, Yugoslavized form. The end product was to be a new supersystem, known as the "socialist market economy" and intended to attract the attention of other socialist countries, especially Yugoslavia's nonaligned friends in the Third World.

The 1965 reforms proved defective for several reasons. First, the market system, which the Yugoslavs practiced in a socialist manner (that is, without genuine competition and without market signals used as a criterion), created serious inequalities not only among individual parts of the country (the north-south dilemma) but also among the same economic branches in different regions and among the workers employed in them. This in turn aggravated ethnic relations since individual nationalities usually begin blaming each other for economic failures when no "real culprits" (that is, the central state and party apparatuses) can be made responsible.[1] Only three years after the economic reforms were announced, protesting students in June 1968 demanded: (1) that all social inequalities should be ended; (2) that the burden of the economic reforms should not be placed on the working class and the poor alone;

(3) that radical socialist democracy right up to the top should be introduced; and (4) that the laissez-faire socialist economy should be abolished.[2]

Rejected in 1968 as ultra-leftist illusions, these four demands were accepted by the regime in 1972. But this acceptance was half-hearted, as has been the case with most major reforms provoked by serious difficulties on the part of the regime. In each case, change was implemented through a campaign, which usually lasted only briefly—until the leaders could consolidate their position. The center, with Tito as its symbol, developed a rather successful strategy of striking first at the left-wingers and then at the right-wingers (sometimes both at the same time) in an attempt to maintain equilibrium. After a brief period of superficial stabilization, the problems reappeared in a more serious form, however, thus heralding a new era of destabilization in all spheres of life, but especially in relations among the different nationalities and republics. The central party and state apparatus then had to intervene again, usually through the form of "Tito's letters." Instead of insisting on the proper implementation of hundreds of laws originally vaunted as the best Yugoslavia ever had, Yugoslav leaders believed that a short but direct letter from Tito to party members would encourage a positive trend in an extremely complicated political and economic system. This was known in Yugoslavia as "letter democracy," in which commands from above replaced (at least for a while) the self-management rules and the country's laws. As a result, the macroeconomic stabilization measures necessary for any successful move in the market system were ineffective against the massive governmental interference designed to prevent the victory of *stihija* (development beyond the control of governmental organizations). The economy in general and individual enterprises in particular began to deteriorate seriously.

Thus, for instance, in the first half of 1978 total losses for thousands of Yugoslav enterprises amounted to some U.S. $600 million. This was said to be a 6-percent increase over 1977.[3] In addition, more than $150 million was thrown away in the form of so-called costs for representation (hospitality and entertainment for customers).[4] Of this $600 million loss, $180 million was produced in Croatia,[5] $107 million in Bosnia-Herzegovina,[6] $76 million in Serbia proper,[7] and $55 million in Montenegro,[8] of which the Aluminum Combine in Titograd alone was responsible for more than $8 million, a threefold increase over 1977.[9] Smaller losses were incurred in Macedonia, Vojvodina, Kosovo, and Slovenia.

According to official statistics published in September 1979, in the first eight months of that year imports grew by 13 percent and exports increased by only 1 percent. As a result, the trade deficit reached $4.3 billion. Only 48.3 percent of imports were covered by exports. The inflation figure for 1979 was estimated in October to be 30 percent,[10] and the increase in admitted losses reached an average of 25 percent (Vojvodina 43 percent; Croatia 41 percent; Bosnia-Herzegovina 32 percent; Slovenia 15.3 percent; Serbia proper 14.6 percent; and Macedonia 13.3 percent). The increase in losses compared with 1978 in Kosovo and Montenegro must have been high since they were not mentioned, except to say that in these two areas "the sum of losses has decreased." According to Branko Čolanović, director of Belgrade's Yugoslav United Bank, Yugoslavia's foreign debt at the end of 1977 stood at some $9.5 billion, and its external credits were estimated at $1.1 billion, resulting in a net foreign debt of $8.4 billion.[11] The trade deficit in that year amounted to $4.3 billion.

Compensating these huge sums were about $1.0 billion in tourist receipts[12] and roughly $2.8 billion in remittances in 1978 from workers abroad.[13] Since the trade deficit in the first eight months of 1979 was some $4.3 billion, however, the revenues from tourist income and remittances from the over 700,000 Yugoslav citizens working in Western Europe (1,100,000 including dependents) would probably not have covered it.[14] Consequently, as of October 1978, over 600,000 of the 5 million workers[15] in the socialist sector received the minimum wage (in Serbia, Montenegro, and Kosovo, 55 percent and in Bosnia-Herzegovina 50 percent of the average monthly salary).[16] In the first three months of 1978, the average wage was about $260,[17] which means that the 600,000 workers employed in enterprises running at a loss received between $130 and $150 per month. (In some cases [varying from branch to branch and from republic to republic], local authorities were empowered to increase the minimum wage, especially for highly qualified and skilled workers, in order to prevent their emigration.)

In addition to the 600,000 workers receiving the minimum wage, there were in 1978 more than 200,000 people for whom rehabilitation was the only answer.[18] In other words, the enterprises in which they worked had to be totally overhauled by the state, a special socialist form of bankruptcy proceedings (no enterprise, in fact, actually went bankrupt). For this purpose, the authorities used funds from enterprises running at a profit. The case of the Industry of Machines and Tractors (IMT) in Belgrade, one of Yugoslavia's major auto plants, is a most instructive example of how such a "Potemkin village"—to use the words of the Belgrade weekly *NIN*—became a victim of a defective economic system. In the first six months of 1978, 3.0 billion dinar (about $167 million) was invested in the IMT. Of this sum only 33 million dinar (about 1.8 million) was available to improve production, introduce new technology, and increase productivity. The remaining 89 percent was spent on things that had little or nothing to do with the actual improvement of the plant. Moreover, at the very time the IMT was struggling against bankruptcy, the International Institute for Development in Geneva mentioned this enterprise among those firms "with an extraordinarily high level of labor productivity." This recognition was based on an official Yugoslav report from Belgrade.

How was it possible that economic accumulation in the IMT dropped to an amazing 1 percent; that is, only 1 of every 100 dinar invested was used to promote production or introduce new technology? According to other (nonembellished) official Yugoslav data, the IMT had to pay most of the squandered money to the state in the form of regular and extra taxes to finance various "common and general social needs," that is, for "noneconomic social consumption."[19] All this, again according to an official admission, demonstrated "that we have found ourselves in an exceptional situation of consumer psychology." A commentator complained that "much more has been spent on nonproductive" branches of the economy than on productive ones, allegedly because full-fledged "competition in consumption must be encouraged" at all levels, a competition that "from time to time assumes the form of sheer waste." In this connection, Prof. Aleksandar Vasić of Belgrade University was quoted as saying that "in the past ten years [1969–1978] all forms of consumption (personal and general) have been, on average, 6 percent higher than the growth in social product; somebody has been spending funds that did not belong to him."[20]

MARXIST PHRASEOLOGY—
NON-MARXIST PRACTICE

Yugoslav party and state leaders seldom gloss over the country's economic difficulties. True, official reports, far from being helpful, usually begin by emphasizing the "dynamic development" and "great successes" of all economic spheres (with the possible exception of agriculture). They do not, however, conceal the negative aspects of the economy: persistent inflation, low labor productivity, huge unemployment figures (785,000 in September 1979),[21] serious losses in thousands of Yugoslav enterprises, and high foreign indebtedness. Yugoslav leaders usually ascribe the "main cause of economic instability"—as Presidium member Branko Mikulić said in a report to the eighth plenary session of the LCY Central Committee on 18 October 1979—to workers' lack of power to make decisions; these are made by "technobureaucrats," who are to be blamed for the ever increasing inflation.

The principal intent of western credits was to promote economic growth. Because the annual installments to be paid to creditors grew to 20 percent of the total credits granted, newly acquired credits have been used mainly to pay the interest on previous loans.

Yugoslav media usually attribute the causes of these economic problems to violations of the self-management rules in general and to violations of the November 1976 Law on Associated Labor in particular. Very seldom, if at all, have domestic analysts dared blame the system as such. When the system is criticized, it is taken to task only indirectly. In December 1971, only ten days after Tito organized radical purges in Croatia on the pretext that "bourgeois and nationalistic elements" had to be prevented from carrying out their "counterrevolution," a Croat professor working in Belgrade, Branko Horvat, said at a symposium that he had "great doubts whether scientific socialism makes any sense." Professor Horvat questioned why people were organizing revolutions and replied that one of the major reasons was the struggle against social inequality. In his opinion, a socialist revolution was necessary because a bourgeois revolution was incapable of solving the problem of social inequality despite the slogan of liberty, equality, and fraternity. "We are also," Professor Horvat continued,

> for liberty, equality, and fraternity—but what has happened? In trying to promote these ideas, we have not created a society of liberty, equality, and fraternity, but rather another type of bourgeois society, and we know what it looks like . . . This means that the socialist revolution, like the bourgeois revolution, has failed to solve these problems too. Should we now, as a result, organize a third kind of revolution that would again proclaim those high humanist ideals and aims without implementing them?[22]

Professor Horvat is not alone in harboring doubts about the value of scientific socialism or creative Marxism. So do the majority of Yugoslav economists, especially the younger ones. In Yugoslavia it is a public secret that those enterprises making a profit became successful only after abandoning, partially or completely, Marxist economic principles in their business practice. But this does not prevent Yugoslavs from continuing to employ Marxist phraseology in justifying their non-Marxist or even anti-Marxist conduct. This combination of Marxist phraseology and non-Marxist practice is one of the most important elements of the Yugoslav socialist market economy. A description by a Russian dissident, Prof. Aleksandr Zinoviev, of the situation in the Soviet Union is equally valid for Yugoslavia: "In a short time, even the most stupid Soviet citizen can learn to manipulate Marxist phraseology so skillfully that in the end it would be difficult to tell the difference between him and a classical Marxist."[23]

In the case of the Yugoslav economic system, for example, Marxist terminology has been lavishly used at all levels in connection with the question of whether the serious difficulties prevailing in the economic system have been full-fledged "conflicts" or only "contradictions." According to one Yugoslav school of thought, contradictions are unavoidably present in all economic systems. They may become conflicts, which are defined as the product of a clash between "two or more opposing interests" within society.[24] Yugoslav writers have in this context quoted Mao Zedong's dictum: "The world consists of contradictions and that without contradictions the world would cease to exist."[25] In other words, contradictions must be tolerated. Unlike Soviet-type societies, which, it is claimed, are free of conflict, Yugoslav writers admit that Yugoslav society has had conflict. Most of them, however, believe that their country has been plagued more by contradictions than by conflicts. In their opinion contradictions and conflicts can be either resolved or relativized, but in both cases only within a system of "self-management agreements and social compacts." They also stress that certain serious conflicts cannot be resolved but only relativized, or reduced to a minimum.

Yugoslavia's economic difficulties, of which the losses in thousands of enterprises are only one aspect, are both contradictions and conflicts. The latter "stem from the character of the ownership of the means of production."[26] Yugoslav theory teaches that state (as in Soviet-type systems) or private (as in the West) control of the means of production automatically provokes conflict in all spheres of life, especially in the economy. Only the system of social ownership prevailing in Yugoslavia has abolished "all kinds of monopoly over the means of production."[27] According to the Belgrade theorist Žarko Papić, by excluding appropria-

tion based on ownership monopoly, "social ownership, because it cannot
be realized economically, is not ownership in the economic sense; in this
sphere it develops as nonownership."[28] It is surprising, therefore, to read
in the Yugoslav media that in Yugoslavia, too, despite the social
ownership system operating in the country since June 1950, conflicts
continue to exist. Unlike the Soviet case, Yugoslav workers themselves,
"associated freely" in self-management production units, control access
to the means of production and in addition receive preference in the
distribution of the products of those means. Workers in Yugoslavia are
not the owners of the enterprises in which they work but rather the
managers or, to be more precise, self-managers.

One gains the impression that some Yugoslav leaders (notably Kardelj)
have carefully read James Burnham's thesis about a "managerial society"
in which the concept of separation of ownership and control has no
sociological meaning: "Ownership means control; if there is no control,
then there is no ownership."[29] The November 1976 Law on Associated
Labor contains many of Burnham's ideas, although Yugoslav theorists
firmly reject any suggestion of their indebtedness to his works, especially
his ideas that those who control are the owners and that "the managerial
economy is in actuality the basis for a new kind of exploiting, class
society." Writing in 1941, Burnham could not have anticipated Tito's
self-management system of 1950. In reading this work, however, one
might think that Burnham had in mind the Titoist system, described in
1956 by Milovan Djilas in *The New Class* as an "exploiting, class society."
Burnham explained the term "exploiting economy" as an economy in
which "one group receives a relatively larger share of the products of the
economy than another," a definition that fits not only the Soviet Union
but also Tito's Yugoslavia.[30]

SHORT- AND LONG-TERM INTERESTS

The official Yugoslav thesis is that in Yugoslavia there is neither state
nor private ownership of the means of production (with the exception of
agriculture since 85 percent of land is held privately) but rather only
social ownership. Why then is Yugoslavia confronted with so many
serious conflicts in its economy and other spheres of life? Here we
encounter a situation similar to the discovery of a drug that successfully
treats, say, stomach cancer but at the same time destroys healthy tissue.
Yugoslav theorists claim that the country has successfully resolved the

problem of the distribution of the means of production (a problem that "tortures" capitalist countries). The Law on Associated Labor, it is said, has eliminated this problem by giving workers preferential treatment in the disposition of income. At the same time, the law has created two other problems. The first arose when workers were given the right to decide freely the disposition of the income they produced—in Yugoslav parlance "to manage the extensive reproduction"—namely, a clash between "the short-term and long-term interests of the working people." Yugoslav workers seem to understand their rights in a self-management society in a Burnhamian way; that is, control of access is decisive and, when consolidated, cannot avoid entailing control over preferential treatment in distribution. (Yugoslav theorists, notably Kardelj, have not agreed with this; see chapter 3.) Hence, conflicts emerging from the clash between workers' short-term (their wages) and long-term interests (the future of their enterprise, region, or the country as a whole) must be either totally resolved (by convincing the workers that they should sacrifice the present in the expectation of a brighter future for their children) or at least relativized, or reduced to a bearable minimum.

The second major problem stemming from the system of socially owned means of production is reflected in the efforts made to establish satisfactorily the degree to which each individual worker contributes to "the process of achieving common income,"[31] that is, the profitability of each person's work. In Yugoslavia—despite the incessant talk about workers' self-management—the workers have not been allowed to assess this themselves. Rather it is done by managerial groups (the technocrats or technobureaucrats) in enterprises. Professor Miladin Korać, a leading Yugoslav sociologist, suggested that throughout an enterprise workers should be paid different wages, "according to each person's individual contribution to achieving the common income."[32] But since the workers are self-managers and themselves control the means of production, who then determines each worker's "individual contribution" and the pay that he should receive for it? This problem has not been resolved. Consequently, despite the many solemn promises given over the past 25 years, implementing the proclaimed principle that a worker should be paid according to work done has been impossible. As a result, thousands of enterprises have run into various major and minor difficulties, many of them—as we have seen—producing huge losses that must be subsidized with funds taken from profitable concerns. In these enterprises the workers were never asked whether they were willing to sacrifice their short-term interests in order to help bankrupt enterprises survive and thus promote their own long-term interests.

These two problems, emerging from the conflict between the idea (and practice) of social ownership and the workers' short-term and long-term interests, have made the viability of the self-management system questionable. This is, of course, only one of the conflicts in the Yugoslav economic system. Yugoslav theorists have listed four other conflicts, which are not directly related to the idea of "social ownership" but have still greatly influenced the development of the country: (1) that between the developed and underdeveloped regions of the country; (2) those stemming from the triangle: employment–specialization of production–foreign trade; (3) that between the idea (and practice) of consumption and economic accumulation (at all levels of society); and (4) that between personal and general consumption.[33]

THE PARTY AND THE WORKERS

"Any reform that involves both the monopoly of power [of the ruling communist party] and the most important branches of production," said Milovan Djilas in a 1978 analysis of the problems of the communist regime in the Soviet Union, "must, in a very short time, lead to the disintegration and decay of the system as a whole."[34] But his (in fact de Tocqueville's) observation can be applied to all communist regimes, including Tito's. In discussing the "signs of decay" in the Soviet Union ("ideological sterility, the inefficiency of the economic system, demands for reforms, the emergence of centrifugal forces"), Djilas indirectly raised the question of their existence in Yugoslavia. Have the reforms implemented since 1950 endangered the LCY's monopoly of power and "the majority of the most important branches of production"? Since the reforms have thus far not led to the system's disintegration, we can infer that they have not been extensive enough. In fact, Yugoslav leaders have always successfully prevented the full implementation of their own reforms. Whenever they felt that a reform was beginning to threaten their monopoly of power, they replaced it with a new reform, justifying their action by quoting the last sentence in the LCY program of April 1958: "Nothing that has been created should be so sacred to us that it cannot be transcended and superseded by something still freer, more progressive, and more humane."[35] Kardelj called this "the permanent revolutionary practice of change." The main reason for the failure of the reforms has not been the reforms per se, but rather the confused theory on which the reforms were based.

Under this method of implementing reforms, Yugoslav workers have been compelled to fight a battle not only between their short-term and their long-term interests, but also against the Yugoslav managerial class and, even more importantly, against the party. Workers have been able to demonstrate their dissatisfaction with the system only through striking. Yugoslavia is the only communist state in which strikes are neither permitted nor forbidden. Rather they are tolerated. Between the first workers' strike in January 1958 (in Slovenia) and the end of 1978, there were several thousand strikes throughout the country.

Yugoslavia's greatest expert on strikes is Neca Jovanov, a Serb from Vojvodina, whose 1976 doctoral dissertation is entitled "Workers' Strikes in the Socialist Federative Republic of Yugoslavia Between 1958 and 1969." Jovanov is secretary of the Trade Union Confederation's Commission on the Political System and Political-Organizational Development of Trade Unions. Judging from several courageous interviews in the second half of 1978, Jovanov can be considered one of the most valuable analysts of conditions among Yugoslav workers.

The first person (in April 1964), however, to call on Yugoslav workers to pressure the government and the trade unions in order to achieve the rights provided them by the self-management system was President Tito.[36] Other Yugoslav state and party officials, like Jovanov, have also demonstrated their sympathy for striking workers. For instance, a party official from Zagreb admitted that workers had been striking because they were "dissatisfied" with the implementation of self-management principles:

> The moment workers feel that someone is manipulating them, that they are not in a position to resolve existing problems according to the principles of self-management, they strike in order to force social and political forces not only in their own enterprises but also outside them to resolve existing problems.[37]

Like Jovanov, this official believed that in organizing strikes "our working people are not against the self-management system" but rather "against all deviations." Jovanov, however, is the only senior Yugoslav official who has not only publicly defended strikes but has also objectively explained their occurrence despite the concept of social ownership and the existence of the self-management system.

STRIKES AND TECHNOBUREAUCRATS

Jovanov (popularly known as the "doctor for strikes") blames "techno-bureaucratic forces" and party organizations and trade unions for the dissatisfaction that workers are voicing. Jovanov bravely criticizes party organizations for preventing the proper implementation of the self-management system as provided in the Law on Associated Labor and in the constitution. Party and trade union officials, Jovanov stresses, have simply turned the self-management system into an institution outside the control of the working class. Technocrats in individual enterprises have pushed workers aside and taken over management, basing themselves on "hierarchical structures." This

> has resulted in a very interesting process: people from what we call hierarchical structures [the bureaucracy] have begun installing themselves in the self-management structure of society and assuming key positions in it, something that was not expected. This is why, in a relatively short time, the number of workers in workers' councils has dropped to only 55 percent while technocrats have gained a decisive influence in them. A paradoxical situation has arisen: workers' councils have begun strengthening their position as institutions, but their social composition does not consist of (and their influence does not derive from) workers. This is why members of workers' councils have been among those who went on strike.[38]

Jovanov claims that workers' influence has decreased at all levels, from workers' councils to the Federal Assembly in Belgrade, party organizations, and trade unions. In his opinion, "the most important reason why we now have more strikes than in the past is that almost nothing has been done to change the basis for distributing economic power to benefit the working class." The situation "hardly differs from that of ten or more years ago," and "the domination of the financial capital concentrated in the banks and to a lesser extent the domination of foreign trade and domestic trade capital in general, compared with the economy at large, have not been touched at all," all this despite the radical reforms previously mentioned. For instance, the ratio between the earnings of ordinary factory workers and those of bank employees is 1:15 or even 1:25. Jovanov cites an illuminating example:

> We visited a bank and asked how long at most a worker employed there must wait to get an apartment? They answered: three years . . . We asked this same question in a shipbuilding enterprise. We were told that there

a worker had to wait at least eighteen to twenty years for an apartment. In a textile factory, we were told that workers there had no chance of getting an apartment during their employment. As you see, the problem is not the economic crisis but rather the distribution of economic power, which is at the expense of the workers.[39]

As a result only "production workers" have ever gone on strike, and those employed in banks, trade, the bureaucracy, and "political organizations" have never done so. In answer to the question of why workers usually approve all regulations presented to them and then later strike against them, Jovanov replied that it was essential to understand that "we are still constrained by an extremely utopian idea, namely the conviction that self-management means that all of us must decide everything." This thesis "about workers as universal self-managers . . . has slowly but surely turned workers into universal ignoramuses."[40] Jovanov then explained that teams of experts in enterprises—specialists, economists charged with distribution, planning, investment, and so on—worked out various plans and projects, amounting to hundreds of pages, and presented them for acceptance or rejection to ordinary workers on workers' councils. These workers then had to reach decisions very quickly; after eight hours at their machines, they were incapable of making proper decisions. "I am a doctor, but I confess that I could not do this after eight hours of work," Jovanov said. His solution is to "abandon the idea of workers as 'universal self-managers' . . . otherwise we will destroy self-management as a principle." He further differentiates between "decision making" and "voting." Workers in Yugoslavia, he claims, are mainly required to vote for or against something rather than to make decisions.

In another interview, Jovanov said that, theoretically, workers in Yugoslavia were promised freedom in disposing of an enterprise's "entire income, but instead practically have to fight to get their own wages." This had so reduced workers to "physical exhaustion that they no longer have the nerve to fight something against which they are powerless, despite all our declarations and political documents." His description of how "political activists" have been handling the quasi-self-management system is instructive.

> You probably know how all this works. An enterprise director has a meeting with two or three of his deputies, the party secretary, and the presidents of the trade union organization and the workers' council. The director then suggests what they call the political line will be. In actual fact this is a ready-made decision since the president of the workers' council

leaves the meeting obligated to get the [director's] decision accepted by the workers' council; the party secretary undertakes to give this decision moral and political support; the same goes for the union president. The director and his team, who have actually made the decision, wait apart while all the political and self-management agencies torment themselves over legalizing the decision. Thus, the whole of political and self-management life is reduced to the point where workers must vote either for or against such a decision. If one of them tries to protest, he is immediately accused of being against self-management (because the workers' council accepted the decision) or against the party (because the party supported it).[41]

Thus, the real reason for workers' strikes and the poor state of the country's economy seems to be that "technobureaucratic absolutism," as Kardelj called it, has imposed itself upon the self-management system. The technobureaucratic managerial class in Yugoslavia, very like the one described by James Burnham, has turned the self-management system into its own instrument. "Theory and practice," said Jovanov in one of his interviews, "have demonstrated hundreds of times that people who are in a position to take the initiative in imposing their own topics for discussion and formulating the proposals for a decision are, in fact, the real decision makers." For instance, 95 percent of all topics dealt with at meetings of the communal assemblies were actually forced on them by governmental and party organizations, he said.[42]

The inadequate implementation of the self-management system has therefore resulted in a contradiction. On the one hand, workers have been encouraged to exercise "radical criticism" and transcend their own existence as hired laborers, the system of state ownership, the party bureaucracy, and the attempt of various privileged groups to revive "capitalist relationships." On the other hand, they have been compelled "to protect their own vital interests and promote their material progress" by using the very elements that they have been encouraged to resist.[43] The party, through its iron embrace of the workers' movement, has promoted workers' self-management. Yet the party is "the sole vehicle for the political power that has promoted modified capitalist relations."[44] The vicious circle is complete.

THREE
The Pluralism
of Self-Management Interests

$\mathbf{E}$dvard Kardelj, Tito's heir apparent until his death on 10 February 1979 in his 69th year, was the chief architect of almost all the party's theories and the country's major laws, most of which Moscow regarded as "Titoist revisionism." This may explain why neither the Soviet party nor the Soviet government sent official delegations to Kardelj's funeral. Not even the Soviet ambassador was present. Yet Kardelj was considered, by Yugoslav Communists at least, one of the "greatest Marxist thinkers" of our era. To appreciate Kardelj's influence, it is enough to mention only the most important of his writings (some coauthored with other Yugoslav leaders): the Law on Workers' Self-Management (1950), the 1958 program of the LCY, the country's last two constitutions (1963 and 1974), the Law on Associated Labor (1976), and finally the book *Roads of Development of the Socialist Self-Management Political System (Pravci razvoja političkog sistema socijalističkog samoupravljanja)*. The last, Kardelj's final work, was the basis of the Eleventh Congress of the LCY, held in Belgrade from 20 to 23 June 1978. In this book Kardelj coined a new term, the "pluralism of self-management interests," which is theme of this chapter.

Kardelj's book is based only partially on the April 1958 LCY program. Changes had been made over the past twenty years in the spirit of the last sentence in the program: "Nothing that has been created should be so sacred to us that it cannot be transcended and superseded by something still freer, more progressive, and more humane."[1] Certainly in theory things have usually been presented as "still freer" and "more progressive," although in practice their appearance has often been quite different.

THE SOVIET VERSUS THE
YUGOSLAV POSITION

Moscow, for its part, has treated the entire compendium of official
Yugoslav ideas as revisionist heresy, regardless of the twists and turns in
formal relations between the Soviet Union and Yugoslavia. The program
of the Communist Party of the Soviet Union (CPSU) adopted at its 22nd
Congress in October 1961, still valid as of 1980, refers twice to "Yugoslav
revisionism" in connection with the LCY program. In chapter 3, "The
World Socialist System," the Soviet party program states: "But the
Yugoslav leaders by their revisionist policy placed Yugoslavia in opposition to the socialist camp and the international communist movement,
thus threatening the loss of the revolutionary gains of the Yugoslav
people." Subsequently the CPSU program emphasizes that "revisionism,
[or] rightist opportunism, which is a reflection of bourgeois influence, is
the chief danger within the communist movement today . . . The ideology
of revisionism is most fully embodied in the program of the League of
Communists of Yugoslavia."[2] Since 1961, despite the changes in Yugoslav-Soviet relations, the Soviets have never revoked the charges made in
this program. They are still used as anti-Tito propaganda in Soviet party
schools.

An excellent illustration of this was the clash between the Russian
Vladimir Gavilevski, the Soviet newspaper *Novoe vremya*'s correspondent
in Yugoslavia, and three Yugoslav party theorists, Miroslav Pečujlić,
Najdan Pašić, and Kiro Hadživasilev. The dispute arose at the end of
September 1977 during a press conference in Belgrade in connection
with the publication of the first version of Kardelj's book on self-
management pluralism. In this book Kardelj claimed that "neither the
state, nor the system, nor any single political party can bring happiness to
man; only man himself can create his own happiness" (p. 14, all
references to this work refer to the second, revised edition). Gavilevski,
who sarcastically described himself as "a representative of the notorious
Novoe vremya," disagreed with Kardelj's treatment of Stalin and Stalinism
and commented: "Stalin died in March 1953, 24 years ago. Yet all
Yugoslav discussions and theoretical debates, as is also noticeable in
Kardelj's latest book, still repeatedly mention so-called Stalinism."[3]
Gavilevski then accused the Yugoslavs of dividing "political systems into
pluralistic and monolithic ones." The former were "good" and the latter

"bad." Gavilevski wanted to know what Yugoslav communist leaders meant by "one-party system," and "whether the Yugoslav participants in this press conference were connecting the one-party system with the Soviet Union, China, or perhaps Mongolia?"

Professor Pašić replied that "as far as Stalin's presence in our discussions is concerned, even 24 years after his death," Stalin "has continued to be an issue" not only in Yugoslavia but also in the Soviet Union. Stalin's ideas were also evident in other communist countries. For a time Stalin had been the leader "of the first country of socialism and even had pretensions to being the fourth classic [figure] of Marxism," after Marx, Engels, and Lenin. When one speaks of Stalin, Pašić said, "one does not necessarily have in mind only the negative aspects of his personality cult, which were criticized even in the Soviet Union." One also thinks of some of Stalin's theoretical concepts—for instance, "Stalin's views about the role of the state"—which are still regarded as valid both in the Soviet Union and some other communist countries. Pašić's reply to Gavilevski's point about Kardelj's alleged appraisal of the multiparty and one-party systems as "good" and "bad" was much sharper, however: "Kardelj has quite clearly and in an explicitly Marxist way criticized multiparty bourgeois parliamentary pluralism. In doing so, Kardelj has dissociated himself from Western interpretations of the one-party system." But Gavilevski was not satisfied with Pašić's answer and continued to insist on being told "which systems were 'good' and which 'bad.' " Pašić reiterated that "it is the business of individual countries and systems and theorists of those countries to explain how much and why they consider themselves either a one-party or a multiparty society." "We wanted to show," Pašić continued, "that the essence of our system was hidden neither in political-parliamentary bourgeois pluralism, nor in a system of monolithic authoritarianism imposed from above in the form of a one-party system."[4]

But the Soviet correspondent's dissatisfaction with Pašić's second explanation forced Professor Pečujlić, the rector of Belgrade University, to intervene. "Kardelj's study cannot and should not be conceived as a kind of Mendeleev's law, as a division into good and bad systems, which would mean labeling each system," Pečujlić said. "On the contrary! We have been criticizing such tendencies in our own country, in our own society, because we consider that neither the one-party nor the multiparty system suits us. In other words, we have been searching for our own road rather than appraising the roads taken by others."[5]

At this point Professor Pašić supported his colleague: "We have never considered our system as being one-party rule in the strict meaning of the term, despite the leading role played by the communist party," especially since self-management was introduced in 1950.

FORMS

According to Kardelj, "ever since the revolution" (1941–1945) Yugoslav Communists have recognized "the need for certain forms of political pluralism." Their starting point was the view that the party should not be a political force that has "a monopolistic control over society, but rather that, as the ideological and political vanguard of the working class, it had a special social role, but one that it could perform only in democratic alliance and in cooperation with all social and democratic forces" (p. 106). Kardelj went even further in his rejection of a party monopoly by claiming that the LCY "is less able than ever to hold any political monopoly or to govern society itself" (p. 206), a claim very similar to Milovan Djilas's views as long ago as 1953. If Kardelj's colleagues were suspicious of any of his ideas, this was certainly true of his insistence that the LCY "should not be the exponent of a one-party system," although they did agree with him that the LCY "was not and never could be a conventional political party, even though it must always see that the crucial levers of power are firmly in the hands of those politically conscious forces that stand on the side of socialism and socialist self-management" (ibid.).

In this respect the Socialist Alliance of the Working People of Yugoslavia (Socijalistički Savez Radnog Naroda Jugoslavije; SAWPY) plays "a specific role." The SAWPY is a front organization with about 13 million members,[6] which includes all mass auxiliary political organizations as well as individuals representing various social groups. According to Kardelj, the SAWPY "is still able to rally all social forces that, regardless of differences in ideology and practical policies, endorse the socialist and self-managing character of our society and its political system" (p. 107). Hence, according to Kardelj, the SAWPY contains all those features of "classical political pluralism that are still needed in our society."

Acting through the SAWPY, the party performs its role as a component part of the system as such "rather than as a force over and above it," as was the case in the past, "although admittedly even now there are still some old ideas harking back to the early days" (ibid.). Kardelj further admitted that in Yugoslavia, in addition to the basic class conflict, there had been "other ideological and political differences and conflicts." However, these differed from the disagreements and conflicts occurring in multiparty and one-party systems. In Yugoslavia they arose "within the context of socialist relations in society" and concerned such questions as the further development of socialist society; the solution of current economic, social welfare, cultural, and other problems; the direction and tempo of the further development of socioeconomic, political, and other relations; and ideological and political differences over the handling of various problems. In contrast with other countries, both Western and Eastern, in Yugoslavia such conflicts and differences "are not resolved" within the context of a "political struggle for power but rather within the system of self-management democracy" (p. 108). In Kardelj's words, "this is why our society cannot favor freedom for political monopolies but must rather promote freedom for self-managers to give voice to their genuine interests in the socialist and self-management society" (ibid.).

Kardelj said that "only such a freedom" might secure the fulfillment of the long-range historical interests of the working class. In fact, the future development of Yugoslav society "must be based on the gradual overcoming of the *pluralism of political monopolies* in favor of a genuine *self-management political pluralism.*" By recognizing that Yugoslav society was "neither monolithic nor amorphous," Kardelj admitted the existence of "different interests determined by sociohistorical facts." Of course, these interests are not those "of the counterrevolutionary remnants" or "the dogmatic champions of a technobureaucratic monopoly based on the ideology of state ownership" that prevails in the Soviet Union and other East European countries. On the other hand, Kardelj admitted that "conflicts of interest" existed in Yugoslavia, especially those that stem from the formula that income should be distributed "according to the work done." These conflicts, however, do not imply "a class differentiation within the working class." Rather they relate to differences in "individual prosperity and social standing" arising within a system of income distribution according to work done. Such a system creates various social differences, "but they are not so great as to cause disunity within the working class" (p. 109).

THE INTERESTS

In Kardelj's view, the LCY is obliged to prevent any such disunity, especially in cases where conflicts become class conflicts between the working class and that section of it that Marx called "the working class's own bureaucracy." Kardelj denied Djilas's 1957 claim that this conflict "by itself" had turned the bureaucracy into a "new class" but admitted that "it does inject elements of a wage-labor or class relationship into production relations" (ibid.). For Kardelj, this is the "real conflict" in contemporary socialism; namely, "the conflict between Stalinist dogmatism and democratic and creative revolutionary Marxist thought." On the other hand, Kardelj also strongly rejected the political pluralism of the Western parliamentary system since it is in sharp opposition to the self-management system. Kardelj listed six main areas in which his "democratic pluralism of self-management interests" is evidenced:

1. "Associated labor" (enterprises) in all its aspects, in conjunction with all forms of individual labor by peasants, artisans, professionals, etc. The interests of these groups are expressed in the form of workers' self-management "in all domains of associated labor."

2. Working people and citizens in public services, such as public health, social welfare, education, science, culture, etc. In this area self-management interests are democratically organized in the form of "self-managing interest communities."

3. Living conditions. This area is the concern of local self-managing communities and self-managing communes.

4. Individual nationalities (in Yugoslavia called "the nations and nationalities"; the latter is the name for ethnic minorities). Their specific interests are guaranteed by the autonomy of the six constituent republics and the two autonomous provinces and by self-managing democratic relations within the federal system.

5. Forces "in the realm of ideology and politics in general," that is, the party and "other" political organizations, such as the SAWPY, trade unions, and youth organizations.

6. "A wide range of common public interests," dealt with in various state (governmental) organs and assemblies formed on the basis of the system of delegations.

Kardelj admitted that each of these realms of self-management interests represents a complicated democratic system of its own. Each is based on self-management organizations rather than "on the hierarchy of a technological organization of labor or business operations" (pp. 110–11).

Kardelj admitted, however, that "in practice, these relations have still not become a complete reality" because the country's "complex social structure" and "clashes between different interests" have not only prevented the development of the desired relations "but have also distorted them." Consequently, Kardelj suggested, "time, experience, knowledge, and a new mentality are needed" in order to bring about this "revolutionary transformation" (p. 111).

KARDELJ'S PARADOXES

The Soviet-Yugoslav dispute over good and bad systems, illustrated by the ideological skirmish between Gavilevski and the three prominent Yugoslav party theorists, and Kardelj's six points dealing with the meaning of "self-management pluralism" do not give a complete picture of events in Yugoslavia in this field. The late 1970s theoretical discussion concerning the "new role" of the party has had a long history. It dates back to the party's Sixth Congress in November 1952 when the Communist Party of Yugoslavia (CPY) changed its name to League of Communists of Yugoslavia. At that time Milovan Djilas was made responsible for introducing a new theoretical concept: the primacy of the party's educational over its commanding role. In order to symbolize this basic reform in the party structure and operation, the Sixth Congress decided to change the party's name. In an article in *Borba* of 4 January 1954, Djilas explained that the LCY "would gradually take on the character of a strong, ideological, widely diffused nucleus, but would lose its party character." The role of personality would grow, on the basis of its quality and its function among the masses "and not only on the basis of its position in the party committee or administration." Although in 1952 Tito and his chief aides supported Djilas's theories, in January 1954 Djilas was purged for the revisionism that he had preached between 1952 and 1954. After Djilas's purge, however, changes in accordance with his ideas continued, and the new party program accepted at the Seventh Congress in April 1958 closely resembled the Djilas line. Since then, there have been several phases, some of them marked by liberal, some by antiliberal activities.

The preparations for the Eleventh Congress of the LCY (June 1978) and the activities that followed clearly indicated the beginning of a new phase in party life. Kardelj's book was its basis. In it one finds so many of the theses that Djilas had preached between 1952 and 1954 that one

must regard Kardelj's work as an ideological rehabilitation of Djilas. This
applies, of course, only to some of its sections. In others, one might
consider it a rehabilitation of Aleksandar Ranković, the secret police
chief purged in June 1966. Kardelj's book contains propaganda for both
extremes, although liberal views prevail. For instance, Kardelj wrote that

> the League of Communists is less able than ever to hold any political
> monopoly or to govern society itself . . . Therefore, the LCY must not be a
> kind of commanding force outside the system of self-management, nor
> should it pull the strings operating the system without taking the responsi-
> bility for it, although there are many in this country who would like to see
> it do so [p. 206].

But elsewhere Kardelj apparently says quite the opposite; namely,
that without the party's monopoly and state interference the system
could not survive. "Despite the withering away of individual functions
performed by the state in favor of the socialist self-management system,
the state authorities still represent a condition of and are an inevitable
instrument for the survival of the self-management system" (p. 37).
Elsewhere, however Kardelj claims that without "state organs . . . the
democratic system cannot exist at all" (p. 120).

Let us examine briefly the liberal side of Kardelj's ideas. One has only
to reread Djilas's article "League or Party," published in the party
newspaper *Borba* on 4 January 1954, to see that Kardelj not only
followed the spirit of this article but even used some of its formulations.
This is true not only of Djilas's claim that the problem was "whether the
League of Communists is to remain the party in the old, prewar, pre-
Cominform, and post–Sixth Congress sense" (that is, occupying more
an educational than a commanding role) but also of Djilas's insistence
that "without Communists there would be no Yugoslavia." Djilas, of
course, changed his mind about the latter claim, although Kardelj and
his colleagues continued to adhere to it. What they share, however, is the
fear that the Yugoslav party will not survive future developments if it
remains a commanding party, unready to compromise; it should instead
remain (in Kardelj's words) "consistent and determined in the struggle
against the real enemies of socialism." Kardelj then adds an important
proviso: "But it must also be prepared to make compromises and follow
a flexible policy when a conflict of interests within self-management
democracy occurs or when the social consciousness of the working
masses falls short of the desired level" (p. 204).

THE MOST PROGRESSIVE SYSTEM

The most difficult explanation Kardelj and his followers attempted concerns the idea that Yugoslavia's one-party system is not an "ordinary" one-party system, even though the LCY must remain the only ruler, at least as long as "antisocialist and anti-self-management forces" are alive. According to Kardelj, "our political system, far from being a one-party system, actually precludes any such system, just as it rejects the multiparty pluralism of bourgeois society." The self-management system cannot tolerate political monopoly "by any force," even though it survives only because of features of a one-party system such as prevail elsewhere in Eastern Europe. In other words, those elements of the one-party system that still obtain in Yugoslavia have been only "an instrument to defend the survival and further development of our self-managing and democratically integrated socialist society" (p. 72), rather than the LCY's ultimate goal. In fact, the one-party system is nothing "but a variant" of the "bourgeois parliamentary system" (ibid.), which means that in both Western capitalist countries and Eastern socialist countries two variants of one and the same "bourgeois parliamentary system" have been operating. According to Kardelj's formulation,

> by maintaining a critical attitude toward the parliamentary system, we are in fact expressing our ideological, theoretical, and practical rejection of bourgeois society's political system, although this same system has been adopted in part by the socialist state in the transitional phases of socialism, either in its one-party or in its multiparty variant [p. 73].

True, Kardelj emphasizes that Yugoslav Communists prefer not to debate these two variants "from the standpoint of ideological exclusiveness" because both systems have frequently played "a very progressive role" in history. Yet one cannot approach party pluralism in a country with a bourgeois parliamentary system in the same way as in a country with its "one-party variant." The latter is, without doubt, more progressive than the former. In countries where socialism "triumphed following an armed revolution," the return to "political pluralism of the parliamentary type would entail a return to the old social antagonisms." For this reason neither of the two variants suits the "higher phase" of socialist construction in Yugoslavia—namely, the self-management system. Certainly, Yugoslav Communists have never been willing "to export their type of socialist revolution," but neither have they been prepared "to import models that do not meet the requirements of our self-management and democratic socialist society" (p. 74). Fortunately, Kardelj says, "there are many democratic systems" in the world "that are and will continue to be more democratic than the bourgeois parliamentary system." On the other hand, he admits that in "contemporary socialist practice" there are also many deficiencies, such as "the reduction of various democratic rights and human liberties," which are justly criticized since no country has a blameless record regarding their observance. Such criticism, in Kardelj's opinion, "serves a progressive purpose, especially when it is aimed at the fascist and other reactionary political systems of the bourgeois state" (p. 75).

However, he firmly rejects the idea that a bourgeois parliamentary system could be grafted onto a "socialist system that emerged from a revolution." Any such attempt is "highly reactionary," especially "when such attempts are directed against a democratic system of socialist self-management such as ours," based on "freedom of self-management." This type of freedom is greater than any freedom granted to people in countries with bourgeois parliamentary systems and certainly more progressive than the freedom prevailing in one-party systems. Even though Kardelj criticizes the one-party system operating in Eastern Europe as incomplete, he still accepts it as "socialist"; it has many defects, of course, but it is certainly "more progressive" than the bourgeois parliamentary system. For Kardelj the problem is not "the political struggle 'for' or 'against' democratic rights and human liberties, but rather a struggle between socialist and antisocialist forces, that is, the struggle between socialist self-management and its opponents" (p. 76).

A DEMOCRATIC DICTATORSHIP

Opponents of the self-management system are to be found, therefore, both in the West and in the East, but the capitalists are more dangerous than fellow socialists. Kardelj says that "freedom of competition to acquire a monopoly of political power" precludes "freedom for self-management." Self-management cannot develop in a one-party system because the ruling party entrusts "the administration of the means of production" to a "managerial apparatus," which de facto usurps the place of the workers as the proper rulers of society (p. 78). The so-called leftist intelligentsia advocate a third way; they would like to see "the Soviet economic system simply 'married' to the American system of democracy in order to create an ideal new society" (p. 77). In Yugoslavia such ideas are advocated by intellectuals who like to call themselves left-wing; but, in fact, these people have been unwilling to accept the self-management system, the essence of which is the system of social ownership and self-management.

Kardelj contrasts the system of social ownership both with the private ownership system found in Western countries and with the state ownership system characteristic of Eastern Europe. The latter was acceptable in the early stages of socialist practice in order to safeguard the passage from one social system to another. Thus, it played a "progressive role" at the very beginning of socialist construction in Eastern Europe, including in Yugoslavia. However, the attempts of Soviet bloc leaders to perpetuate the state ownership system "as an essential principle of socialism" were bound to become a "conservative obstacle" to the progress of socialism. The Yugoslavs regard this as Stalinism and see it embodied in the "technobureaucratic tendencies" stemming from misinterpretations of the dictatorship of the proletariat. Kardelj says that associating the word dictatorship with the notion of violation is wrong, just as identifying the term democracy with the concept of freedom is wrong (p. 80). In his opinion, every state authority is in fact a special form of violation, that is, of dictatorship. This is equally true of the Western parliamentary system. "It is therefore pure political hypocrisy," Kardelj writes, "to accuse a socialist society of lack of democracy and of rule by dictatorship, while saying that bourgeois society is free of dictatorship and is ruled democratically" (ibid.).

Kardelj identifies the coercion practiced in communist countries with that found in Western-style systems. But he also approves the decision by "some [Western European] communist parties" to abandon the term dictatorship of the proletariat since this obliterates the difference existing in theoretical definitions between the bourgeois parliamentary system presented as a democratic system and the socialist system branded as a dictatorial system. Nevertheless, Kardelj hastens to add,

> We have no need to follow in their footsteps. We have stated in all our programs that the sociohistorical essence of political, that is, state, authority in our society is the dictatorship of the proletariat. We included this again in our 1974 constitution, and I think we were right to do so. We certainly do not identify either the bourgeois or the proletarian dictatorships with their means of coercion, which are sometimes more and sometimes less democratic, because severe distortions can also occur in a socialist society during the transitional period [p. 81].

Kardelj's basic claim is that the dictatorship of the proletariat "need not be a dictatorship of the state apparatus, or a state despotism, but is rather a concept of government in which the working class, following its immediate and its long-term historical interests, has the undisputed leading role in society" (p. 82). For this reason, he regards the self-management system as a "special form of the dictatorship of the proletariat" because it does not preclude the democratization of society but rather "guarantees" it. Of course, the leading role of the working class can be exercised either by means of a multiparty or a one-party system provided it is "under the genuine supervision of the workers and the people" (ibid.). He believes that the Yugoslav variety of the dictatorship of the proletariat is reflected in the idea of the "democratic pluralism of self-management interests." Kardelj sees a difference between the coercion implied both in countries with multiparty systems and in those with one-party systems and the coercion implied in Yugoslavia:

> In the Yugoslav system coercion is limited to the struggle against attempts by the remnants of obsolete classes and antisocialist and anti-self-management forces to reimpose the old system on our society and to deprive the working class and working people of the freedom that made it possible for them to fight for the realization of their interests [ibid.].

For Kardelj, "every state represents authority, and as such is a form of dictatorship." Moreover, "democracy as a political system is itself a form of authority and therefore a form of dictatorship" (p. 83). Hence, the long-range objective of socialism in Yugoslavia "should not be to create a state-sponsored democracy, but rather to socialize state functions" by promoting self-management. Under the self-management system, the state apparatus will become a "specialized public service." Of course, the changes that will resolve the manifold contradictions in a socialist state "cannot be brought about overnight," Kardelj says, "nor is it possible for corrective regulations of the state or some other agency concerning relations among people to be superseded quickly" (ibid.). This is especially true of the views of the "ultra-leftist intelligentsia," who rebel against all forms of authoritarian order, against rule and subjugation, and against hierarchy in society, all of which are goals that, in order to be realized, would need "enormous coercive force." "What they want [and here Kardelj is obviously referring to the Communists associated with the banned journal *Praxis*] is a big stick in the hands of an administrative authority . . . a 'tutorial dictatorship.' " Needless to say, the *Praxis* group never advocated such a solution. On the contrary, they stubbornly rejected any state interference. For Kardelj the only answer is the democratic pluralism of self-management interests.

THE HEART OF THE THEORY

Despite the foregoing discussion, it is difficult to envision clearly the meaning of self-management pluralism, especially since Tito and his closest aides seldom, if at all, mentioned Kardelj's theory after his death. In a long speech at the third plenary session of the Central Committee, held in Belgrade on 5 April 1979, the Montenegrin Vidoje Žarković, a member of the Central Committee Presidium and the State Presidency, did not once mention pluralism of self-management interests in describing the idea of collective leadership, even though Kardelj's book had served as the basis for the Eleventh LCY Congress in June 1978.[7] Similarly in a major speech on 19 April 1979 on the occasion of the 60th anniversary of the CPY, Tito said not a word about the pluralism of self-management interests.[8] Finally, in an interview with the Belgrade daily *Borba*, Dr. Vladimir Bakarić discussed many topics but did not mention Kardelj's idea even in passing.[9] One should recall Dr. Bakarić's reply in June 1978 to a question from a West German journalist about Kardelj's concept. Bakarić said he thought that "the whole idea has been misunderstood," a rather unusual comment about a senior colleague from (at that time) the third-ranked man in the state and the party. According to Dr. Bakarić, this misunderstanding arose because

in the West pluralism means the existence of several parties in parliament. However, Yugoslavia does not intend to maintain a parliament containing different parties. It has its own political system based on delegations . . . Of course, there have been many different interests. These interests have nothing to do with any class conflict but could come into conflict with each other . . . This is why Kardelj chose the word "pluralism," because the problem does not concern monolithism—that is, the idea that the Central Committee has to decide alone, and it must be so. This is not the case here . . . In other words, Kardelj used the expression "pluralism" in order to signify that the system is not monolithic and that everybody has the possibility of saying what he likes.[10]

Bakarić's explanation of the misunderstanding and his, Tito's, and Žarković's failure to mention Kardelj's idea indicate some dissatisfaction among top Yugoslav party and state leaders with pluralism of self-management interests. As a result, the idea is no longer widely propagated. Does this mean that Kardelj's theory died with its creator? It is too early to make such a claim since other leading personalities in the Yugoslav party would undoubtedly like to see Kardelj's ideas gain the ascendancy. Žarković's speech at the third plenary session of the Central Committee shows that opposition to the idea of collective leadership also exists, stemming "sometimes from an inability to see the essence of the problem, sometimes from inertia and traditionalism, and sometimes from the fear that the result could be a weakening or loss of monopolistic positions."[11] These people claim, according to Žarković, that affirming collective leadership and collective decision making "might weaken the efficiency of our system." It seems, however, that the very people who now oppose collective leadership also oppose "self-management pluralism," namely, senior officials at the communal, provincial, and republican levels. These are the people who have been called on to implement both Kardelj's theory and, earlier, the concept of collective leadership. In the event, this has meant depriving themselves of power, even though they had been the main pillars of the system. Hence, Žarković spoke of a "long process" and admitted in the conclusion of his speech that abroad "skepticism prevails concerning Yugoslavia's ability to survive on its new course."

This is, in fact, a point on which Žarković also agrees with Kardelj, who saw the development of Yugoslavia's socialist transformation along self-management pluralistic lines as a long process. Kardelj envisioned that future changes in the political structure of society would lead to the acceptance of "new and more advanced forms of democratic life." He prophesied that "new and different forms of democratic ideological and political organizations" would also emerge, of course within the framework of the self-management system (p. 103). But these new forms could in no way be the "conventional political parties" now prevailing in the bourgeois systems: "In other words, in the society of socialist self-management such [political] organizations will have approximately the same position as that enjoyed by organizations in the fields of science, culture, etc., and not a position of monopoly control of political power, such as they have in the system of bourgeois democracy" (ibid.).

Nor is the one-party system operating in the Soviet bloc countries acceptable, which means that the monopoly of power enjoyed by the Yugoslav party must also be abandoned. The main argument of Kardelj's book, therefore, appears to be that pluralism of interests must exist, but that the existence of different parties is prohibited. But, said Kardelj,

> this does not mean that we are or should be hostile to every form of democratic political pluralism. On the contrary, because of the multitude of interests in society arising from class, economic, political, social, and other considerations in the life, work, and creativity of people, it is clear that there can be neither democracy nor human freedom if man is not able to enjoy free expression of his interests and his ideas, of his aspirations and creative views [p. 106].

The only problem for Kardelj was the "forms such political pluralism should take."

The theories preached for the past 30 years in Yugoslavia have not been implemented because the new mentality that Kardelj suggested was necessary to effect change has not been created, nor is there any prospect of it coming into being for a long time to come. Nevertheless, Kardelj believed that in comparing Yugoslavia's communist system with other systems (both communist and noncommunist), one should point not to the system's "momentary weaknesses and shortcomings" but rather to the "prospects for freedom that it envisions." In other words, even though Yugoslav leaders and party theorists stubbornly insist that other systems should be appraised on their current merits, they wish their own system to be judged according to its aspirations.

FOUR

The Yugoslav Army

According to the latest official statistics, the Yugoslav armed forces number 259,000 soldiers, noncommissioned officers, and officers (of whom 145,000 are conscripts). There are 195,000 (130,000 conscripts) in the army; 25,000 (8,000 conscripts) in the navy (including marines); and 44,000 (7,000 conscripts) in the air force. The Yugoslav People's Army (YPA) has about 1,500 tanks and 332 combat aircraft (including 126 MiG-21/F/PF/Ms). Its paramilitary forces and reserves include 500,000 reservists, 16,000 frontier guards, and 1,000,000 territorial defense forces. Defense expenditure in 1979 was 52.47 billion dinars, or about $2.81 billion, compared with an estimated gross national product in 1977 of $37.8 billion.[1] Since the major purges in Croatia in 1971 and in Serbia in 1972, foreign observers have considered the YPA the only potential aspirant capable of assuming control of the country after Tito's death. The highly centralized and hierarchically organized YPA is the only institution in Yugoslavia without self-management. President Tito himself, during the December 1971 purges of Croatian nationalists, referred to the YPA as the last savior of the country and its communist system.

In a 22 December 1971 speech in the small Bosnian town of Rudo on the occasion of the 30th anniversary of the YPA, Tito discussed the problem of Yugoslavia's unity and the YPA's role as the guarantor of that unity.[2] The night before, while addressing a gathering in the Bosnian capital of Sarajevo, Tito had said that the YPA's task is not only to defend the country against foreign aggressors "but also to defend our socialism when we see that it is in danger and that there is no other means of defending it."[3] In his Rudo speech he was even more adamant about the army's role:

There is also the question of the army's role in preserving the achievements of our revolution. Although its primary task is to defend our country against foreign enemies, our army is also called on to defend the achievements of our revolution within the country, should that become necessary. It cannot be otherwise. I say this, although I believe that we have sufficient forces outside the army to be really able to ensure our peaceful development, and I believe that there is no need to fear any great excesses. But if it comes to shooting, the army is also here. This should be made clear to all.[4]

It is important to realize that although the purged Croatian officials were accused of planning various counterrevolutionary activities, especially Croatia's secession from Yugoslavia, the insistence of some that the YPA should be divided into separate republican armies precipitated the purge. In his speech in Rudo, Tito said that those purged had wanted "little by little to take the army into their own, Croatian hands." To stormy applause Tito exclaimed: "They will have to wait a long time for this. I believe that the Sava [a river that runs from Slovenia through Zagreb and flows into the Danube at Belgrade] will first have to start running upstream toward the Triglav [Yugoslavia's highest mountain, in Slovenia] before that happens." Tito added that fortunately for the country "we have rescued our army and preserved it, that we have preserved it from the influence of all elements of the class enemy, that it has remained united at such a high level of consciousness." He warmly praised the party organization in the YPA, "with which I have not the least quarrel." Several months before, in March 1971, Gen. Janko Bobetko, one of the Croats purged in December, had said that Yugoslavia's armed forces "must become a part of self-management society." He made this claim during a session of the Croatian Central Committee, insisting that "society" should acquire "full control" of the army. As long as President Tito was alive, General Bobetko said, there was no reason to harbor any fears about the army's possible political role in the country.[5] But this assertion implied a crucial question: Will this be the case after Tito's death?

CAPITULATION AND TREASON

The role of the YPA has always been controversial. General Bobetko was not alone in voicing suspicions about the army's future role; similar doubts have been expressed by such party leaders as Dr. Vladimir Bakarić. In December 1971, only two weeks after the purge of nationalistic Croatian party and state leaders—a move that Dr. Bakarić staunchly supported—he admitted in an interview with a Western newspaper that the YPA represented "a certain potential danger," although Tito's authority was so great that nobody in Yugoslavia could inherit it, "not even the army." Significantly, Dr. Bakarić seemed uncertain about the army's future plans because he spoke of "the present time" and added: "Any attempt by the army to seize power in Yugoslavia would unleash a civil war."[6] But Bakarić's outspoken comments contradicted Tito's speeches in Sarajevo and Rudo. Tito claimed that the YPA's principal task was to defend the country against foreign enemies and class enemies within the country in order "to defend the achievements of our revolution." But Dr. Bakarić said in his interview: "The army's function is not to maintain internal order within the country but to protect Yugoslavia's frontiers against foreign enemies." Finally, Dr. Bakarić "corrected" foreign claims that 80 percent of the YPA's officer corps were Serbs; the correct figure was "at most 70 percent."

Before the 1971 purges, the Croats openly deplored this Serbian predominance in the YPA. (Even after them, their protests continued, but mutedly.) In early November 1971 a commentary appeared in *Hrvatski tjednik,* the official publication of the Croatian cultural organization Matica Hrvatska, criticizing the draft text of the Croatian constitution for omitting any mention of "the role of the republic in determining national defense policy." The unnamed commentator added that "the constitution should guarantee one of the most basic democratic rights; namely, that a citizen should serve his military term in his own republic and that the language of command in the army should be that of his own people." Finally, the author demanded that "the designation Yugoslav People's Army be changed to Armed Forces of the Socialist Federative Republic of Yugoslavia" because, as the author emphasized, " 'Yugoslav People's Army' was introduced at a time when centralistic-unitaristic tendencies had begun."[7] We have previously observed Tito's strong reaction to these Croatian demands.

Tito and his chief aides firmly opposed any attempt to disrupt Yugoslavia's unity from within. Similarly they adamantly insisted that all attempts to subjugate Yugoslavia from outside would be strongly resisted. This is best demonstrated both in the constitution adopted in February 1974 and in the two laws on national defense, the first adopted in 1969 and the second in 1974. According to Article 238 of the constitution,

No one shall have the right to acknowledge or sign an act of capitulation, or to accept or recognize the occupation of the Socialist Federative Republic of

Yugoslavia or any of its constituent parts. No one shall have the right to prevent citizens of the Socialist Federative Republic of Yugoslavia from fighting an enemy who has invaded the country. Such acts shall be unconstitutional and punishable as high treason. High treason is the gravest crime against the people and shall be punished as a serious criminal act.

The constitution was passed on 21 February 1974. Two months later, on 26 April, the Federal Assembly in Belgrade accepted the new Law on National Defense. Article 7 of this law repeats the first sentence of Article 238 but adds: "No one shall have the right to acknowledge or sign an act of capitulation or surrender of the armed forces or of any part of it."[8]

This discrepancy between the constitution and the Law on National Defense has no particular significance since capitulation of the country means capitulation or surrender of the armed forces. And this is precisely what both documents are designed to prevent. The previous, February 1969, Law on National Defense was urgently passed after the August 1968 invasion of Czechoslovakia when Tito adjudged Yugoslavia's defense capability quite inadequate. The 1969 law proclaimed the Nationwide Defense System (Opštenarodna odbrana; NDS). Its aim is to organize such immediate resistance that "the enemy is never allowed to relax, so that feelings of insecurity, powerlessness, fear, panic and a loss of faith in victory are created in him."[9] Under this system, both the general public and the armed forces must be in a permanent state of emergency, prepared to wage a people's war.

SOCIALIST AGGRESSION

According to Yugoslav military experts, Marx's theory of an armed nation has found its fullest expression in the Yugoslav self-managing socialist system and constitutes the real basis of the NDS. They claim that President Tito successfully used Marx's ideas in creating his strategy of organizing the people for defense "as a function of self-management and the political authority of the working class." Only thus can "the greatest possible guarantee of protection for our socialist community against any possible aggression and against other threats to our peaceful road to progress be provided."[10]

Since the Czechoslovak invasion of August 1968, Yugoslav leaders have feared that a "local" war might be waged against their country. In their opinion this form of war "appears the most likely because of the present correlation of forces, the nuclear balance between the great powers, and the general awareness of the consequences of nuclear war."[11] Yugoslavia's leaders believe that its readiness and strength reduce the probability of an invasion. The Vietnamese invasion of Cambodia (December 1978) and China's subsequent invasion of Vietnam, however, confirmed Yugoslav fears that their country is threatened not only by the imperialists but also by the socialist countries. Many Yugoslavs have made similar statements, but that made in April 1979 by a senior Yugoslav army general deserves special attention. General Džemil Šarac, a Moslem by nationality, who until December 1978 was president of the LCY Committee in the YPA and was later appointed an under secretary in Yugoslavia's Defense Ministry, spoke at the third plenary session of the LCY Central Committee, held in Belgrade on 5 April 1979. General Šarac cautioned would-be aggressors about Yugoslavia's defense preparations and quoted Tito's statement that "it is almost a rule that aggression is not attempted against those countries and those people who are expected to demonstrate strong resistance and where the outcome of a war would be uncertain for the aggressor." General Šarac added that

> Marxism, as we know, does not recognize the export of its model to anyone, especially not at the point of a bayonet . . .

> After World War II, especially in the period between 1948 and 1955, we had Stalin's military threats against socialist Yugoslavia, which has not been prepared to allow itself to be subjugated and does not accept anyone's domination. Later came the military intervention in other socialist countries [Hungary and Czechoslovakia]. And now in Indochina, where socialist countries have been waging war against each other, the armed forces of Vietnam have invaded Cambodia, while the armed forces of China have invaded Vietnam. The conflict between the two largest socialist countries, China and the Soviet Union, threatens to assume even greater proportions. This is why one cannot now ignore the possibility of the creation of various combinations in the formation of alliances between states with similar or different socialist systems in any new wars that might occur in our era.[12]

General Šarac also said that any military pressure or any direct aggression against Yugoslavia would be "antisocialist and counterrevolutionary because this would be aggression against socialist self-managing and independent Yugoslavia, against the achievements of a great authentic socialist revolution, against a prominent fighter for peace and progress in the world." According to General Šarac:

Every country has the right to defend itself against aggression, regardless of which side it comes from . . . Aggression remains aggression, and occupiers remain occupiers, regardless of the flag they wave or the slogans they use to justify their plans for conquest. Armed resistance against any military intervention or aggression is the natural right of every people and every country.[13]

General Šarac accused "individual socialist countries, responsible for military intervention in and aggression against other socialist countries," of behaving according to a pattern "characteristic of imperialist countries." He insisted that all communist countries and parties must be "equal and independent" and that their behavior in this connection "is more important than any proclamation issued by individual countries."

FRATERNAL HELP

The Yugoslav attitude on aggression against their country is quite clear: they are ready to oppose every aggressor with all forces, means, and forms of resistance possible. This view stems—as an article in 1972 made clear—"from the conviction that our readiness and strength will reduce the probability that we will be invaded, and that if we are invaded, we will be able to ensure victory over an aggressor, regardless of his strength."[14]

This is the basis of the 1974 Law on National Defense, which has 231 articles in comparison with 183 in the 1969 law. This law does not specify from which side a possible invasion of Yugoslavia might come, but like General Šarac it states that *any* aggressor would be resisted. The law does not mention, however, what would happen if foreign armed forces are "invited" to lend "fraternal support and help," as happened in Czechoslovakia in August 1968.

Neither the country's constitution nor the federal Law on National Defense nor any of the provincial and republican laws on national defense contains a single word about this problem. In January 1971, eleven months before the purges in Croatia, the Croatian National Assembly (Sabor) published the draft Law on Nationwide Defense, at that time the first such law in Yugoslavia. This draft law—which was never accepted and after the purges was abandoned—contained a new formulation that was was not included in the 1974 federal law. Although Article 238 of Yugoslavia's constitution and Article 7 of the Law on National Defense forbid anyone in the country to accept the capitulation of the country and tolerate its occupation, the second paragraph of Section 4 in the Croatian law's preamble said: "No one has the right to *invite* the enemy's armed forces into the country, to help enemies in carrying out any forcible measures against our citizens, or to collaborate with them in the political and economic field" (emphasis added).[15]

Croatian party and state leaders, who were later purged as nationalists and chauvinists, believed this provision allowed them to disagree beforehand with any possible invitation of enemy armed forces extended by any other Yugoslav constituent republic or nationality. In other words, all Yugoslav republics, provinces, and nationalities would have to decide collectively who was friend and who was foe. This would have been especially true under the rule of a collective state leadership composed of representatives of the various nationalities, as happened after Tito's death. The purged Croatian leaders believed that, in theory, one republic or nationality could consider the Soviets as enemies while another might view them as friends.

It might appear that after the 1971 purges the idea of mentioning the invitation of foreign troops into the country in any of the country's major laws or the constitution was abandoned. In 1973, however, a jointly authored book entitled *How Yugoslavia Would Fight a War* was published in Belgrade. As one Yugoslav reviewer emphasized, "the book fully expressed official views on the character and manner of socialist Yugoslavia."

After mentioning the constitutional provision that "no one shall have the right to acknowledge or sign an act of capitulation," the reviewer quoted another "provision," one that has never been mentioned either in the constitution or in any of the defense laws: "No one shall have the right to invite anyone from outside to interfere in the internal affairs of the Socialist Federative Republic of Yugoslavia."[16] Apparently the reviewer simply invented a nonexistent "official" theory that he wanted to represent as a part of the constitution. Doubtless the problem of invitation has been hanging over the heads of Yugoslav leaders like a sword of Damocles.

THE NATIONWIDE DEFENSE SYSTEM

As we have seen, Yugoslav party and state leaders believe that only strong armed forces can ensure peace and deter all would-be aggressors. Naturally Yugoslav leaders have found it difficult to preach socialist internationalism while trying to persuade the citizenry that the aggressor might come from either the capitalist West or the socialist East. This dilemma is apparent in the concluding paragraph of Section 4 of the preamble of the Law on National Defense: "By firmly defending its self-management road to socialism, the Socialist Federative Republic of Yugoslavia is simultaneously fulfilling its internationalist obligations in constructing a classless society, a society without aggression and wars."[17]

This seemingly innocuous paragraph reveals the basis of Tito's concept of the NDS. First, Yugoslavia's separate road to socialism through self-management is to be continued. Second, contrary to Moscow's thesis against this "separate" system, Yugoslavia and the LCY will fulfill their "internationalist obligations"; that is, they will continue to remain aloof from any form of "national communism," an expression that has never been accepted in Yugoslavia. Third, if aggression comes from the socialist countries, the falsity of their socialism would be revealed since a *real* socialist society is "without aggression and war." This concept was demonstrated by the Vietnamese invasion of Cambodia and the Chinese invasion of Vietnam, and especially by the Soviet invasion of Afghanistan—a nonaligned country.

Of course, the issue here is not the correctness of this thesis—that is not in doubt—but rather the extent to which people in Yugoslavia are prepared, after Tito's death, to accept it. In other words, will any possible offer of fraternal help be interpreted as aggression? Judging from General Šarac's speech before the Central Committee plenum, one is inclined to say yes. In this context, it is worth reproducing in full Section 3 of Article 7 of the Law on National Defense.

> If an enemy has temporarily occupied a part of Yugoslavia's territory, the working people and citizens, the units of the armed forces, agencies of the sociopolitical communities, basic organizations of associated labor [the enterprises], and other self-managing organizations and communities, as well as other sociopolitical and other social organizations, located on that [occupied] territory shall continue the armed struggle and other forms of nationwide resistance against the enemy, shall act according to Yugoslav law, and shall carry out decisions and orders issued by the authorities in charge of leading the nationwide resistance in that part of the [occupied] territory.[18]

In practice, this means that "once the struggle has started, it can only stop when the aggressor has been destroyed or when he has been driven out of the country." For this reason "there can be no bargaining with an aggressor."[19] Although the Yugoslav system of nationwide defense is envisioned as defending the country against foreign aggression, the official theory goes a step further and insists that it has "a defensive character only in global terms" and is not directed against any country that is not an aggressor.

> Actually, however, the concept of nationwide defense is very much an
> *offensive variant* with regard to the way in which struggle is waged because it
> is based on the knowledge that nothing can be achieved through passive
> resistance and that attack is the only way of breaking the power of an
> aggressor and of gaining victory over him.[20]

Another basic principle of the NDS "is to prevent the aggressor from applying blitz warfare techniques on Yugoslavia's battlefields." Yugoslav political and military leaders are aware that contemporary war "is all-embracing and total," but they are convinced "that there is not a single aggressor capable of sending as many soldiers to fight us as we would have armed people waiting for them, not to mention the differences that exist in the fighting spirit, morale, and other values between our soldiers and those of the aggressor, in addition to all our advantages."[21] The Yugoslavs have a high opinion of their own armed forces and feel that any aggressor accustomed to blitz warfare would be wrong in believing that he could easily overrun the country. This is why Yugoslavs warn all would-be aggressors: "Anybody not prepared for considerable bloodshed and a long and arduous war in which their forces would be gradually and ultimately destroyed would be well advised not to start a fight."[22]

The main characteristics of the NDS are "active" as opposed to "futile passive" resistance (an indirect reference to the situation in Czecho-slovakia in August 1968) and resistance by the "entire population" embraced in the YPA and the territorial defense units, who would fight "night and day, in winter and in summer, in fog, rain, and snow." Yugoslav leaders are, of course, aware that preventing an "aggressor from breaking into our country" would be extremely difficult. But "the further the aggressors penetrate, the worse it would be for them," for "no aggressor would be able to impose a purely frontal form of combat." The military leaders of the Yugoslav armed forces and territorial defense units, it is claimed, would be obeyed so strictly that the aggressors would have no opportunity to enjoy any possible temporary successes.

Unlike some other communist countries, which have been doing their utmost to conceal their defense tactics, Yugoslav leaders have been revealing everything in an attempt to persuade both potential aggressors and their own public that any attack against Yugoslavia would be unsuccessful.

THE SUPREME COMMANDER
AFTER TITO

One of the most important factors in the country's defense system is the question of the armed forces' commander-in-chief. As long as President Tito was alive, there was no problem regarding this top military post. In addition to his offices as SFRY and LCY president, Tito was also commander-in-chief of the armed forces. This is explicitly stated in Section 3 of the preamble to the Law on National Defense. Later, sections, however, omit Tito's name when describing the duties of the supreme commander of the armed forces. This is understandable because after his death the collective leadership (the State Presidency) replaced Tito as head of state. This fact makes certain provisions of this law even more complicated.

Article 20 of the Law on National Defense mentions twelve functions of the supreme commander of the armed forces. A special provision in the same article stipulates:

> The supreme commander of the armed forces can transfer the execution of definite actions of commanding and leading the armed forces to the federal secretary for national defense [the defense minister]. In order to execute the functions of the supreme commander of the armed forces and to execute the functions transferred to him by the supreme commander, the federal secretary for national defense can issue regulations, orders, instructions, and other acts.[23]

From the text it would appear that the defense minister in his capacity as deputy supreme commander would himself decide his rights and duties.

Section 4 of Article 105 of the defense law provides that the federation, that is, the top federal authorities, "shall organize and prepare the Yugoslav People's Army and shall lead and *command it*" (emphasis added). This makes the third body to command the armed forces. Moreover, Article 112 makes a fourth body, the State Presidency, responsible for the "realization of nationwide defense."

In addition, the same article provides that "by federal law the composition and organization of the Council for National Defense shall be established, as well as the scope of affairs to be independently executed by the council within the rights and duties of the Presidency of the SFRY." This means that the Council for National Defense would supervise the country's defense in the name of the State Presidency. Finally, the federal government is also responsible for the organization of national defense. Obviously the Federal Secretariat for National Defense (Yugoslavia's defense ministry) plays the principal role here; thirteen articles of the defense law (Articles 114–26) deal with the defense ministry. Since Tito's demise, this ministry has clearly played the most important role in the country's defense, and perhaps even more than that—for it is no easier to visualize collective leadership of the country's defense than it is to imagine self-management in the armed forces.

To further complicate matters, Article 14 provides that the YPA is "a common armed force of all nations and nationalities [national minorities] and of all working people and citizens of the Socialist Federative Republic of Yugoslavia." Yet this article also provides that each of the six constituent republics and two autonomous provinces is to have its own defense ministry that will cooperate with the central defense agencies in Belgrade in organizing the defense of each republic and province. Communes must also contribute to implementing the principles of the NDS.

The section of the Yugoslav constitution (Part 4, Chapter 3) entitled "The President of the Republic" (Articles 333 through 345) automatically laspsed after Tito's death. Chapter 2 (entitled "The Presidency of the Socialist Federative Republic of Yugoslavia") then took effect, for it is obvious that the former position of the president of the republic no longer obtained. In this context differences concerning the command of the armed forces will inevitably arise. Article 335 of the constitution stipulates that "the president of the republic shall be commander-in-chief of the armed forces of the Socialist Federative Republic of Yugoslavia." Article 313, however, which deals with the collective leadership popularly called the State Presidency, stipulates that the State Presidency "is the supreme body in charge of the administration and command of the armed forces of the SFRY in war and peace."

Article 342 provides that the president of the republic "as the commander-in-chief of the armed forces" shall—

1. direct and command the armed forces of the SFRY and determine the fundamentals of plans and preparatory measures for the defense of the country;

2. determine a plan for the use of the armed forces of the SFRY in the event of war and order the use of armed forces in peacetime;

3. appoint, promote, and relieve of duty generals and admirals and other officers, as specified by federal law; and

4. appoint and relieve of office the presidents, judges, and lay-assessors of military courts, and military public prosecutors.

After Tito's death it was intended that some of these duties would be carried out by the State Presidency, which, according to Point 6 of Article 315 of the constitution "shall appoint, promote, and relieve of duty generals and admirals and other army officers" as well as the officials mentioned in Point 4 of Article 342. Article 316, however, provides for a quite different situation after Tito's death. Since the collective leadership cannot "direct and command the armed forces" as the president of the republic did, the State Presidency is authorized "in matters concerning nationwide defense" to lay down "the fundamentals of plans and preparatory measures for the defense of the country, issue guidelines for taking measures to alert and mobilize the country's potential and forces for defense purposes . . . order general or partial mobilization and, if the SFRY Assembly is not in a position to meet, proclaim a state of war."

The most important section of this article is the provision that the State Presidency "may transfer specific affairs concerning the administration and command of the armed forces of the SFRY to the federal secretary of national defense [the defense minister]," who will be responsible to the State Presidency "for the conduct of affairs transferred to him." Another important point is that the State Presidency, "for the purpose of reviewing the implementation of established policy concerning the administration and command of the armed forces . . . may send its delegates to the Federal Secretariat of National Defense and to other higher commands of the SFRY armed forces."

Without question, the role to be played by the Yugoslav defense minister now that Tito is dead will be extremely important. No one can expect civilian authorities to exert any serious control over the armed forces of a country in which the NDS has been elevated to a prerequisite for the state's survival and in which each individual citizen is invited to be first a soldier and only then a political activist—all this in a country where military defense has been proclaimed the foremost political objective.

THE ARMY AND SELF-MANAGEMENT

This state of affairs makes the relation between the self-management system and the YPA one of the country's most crucial issues. Shortly before the purges in Croatia and Serbia, a Bosnian party theorist said that the Yugoslav army was "the most sensitive social institution" in terms of "ideological indoctrination" about the self-management system. He admitted that "the ideologization of the army could be distorted" when turned into "total indoctrination." Moreover, "the military structure, despite all the positive influences social changes have had on it, remains an object of ideologization, that is, of ideological indoctrination, as long as this is required." This means that one "must have sympathy for such a state of consciousness" in those serving in the army.[24]

The conflict between self-management and the army arose because self-management has been a dynamic system while ideology has been static. The army, with its hierarchical organization, has developed passively in contrast to the dynamism of the self-management system, which stems from its democratic (anti-hierarchical) structure. This point is even more apparent when one considers that the army is the only institution in Yugoslavia in which self-management has not been applied. The official response to this is that the development of Yugoslav society as a whole, its self-management basis, and the increasing decentralization in all walks of life could not but influence the army. Hence, the concept of nationwide defense is simultaneously a means of socializing the people's defense and a means of enabling the army to become the strongest force in the state.

Writing in 1970, a Yugoslav army general claimed that there were two ways of "socializing the people's defense": indirectly, through the spontaneous activities of the "armed people"; and directly, by means of state coercion. In the current phase of socialization of the people's defense, the state apparatus prescribes measures to be taken. The second phase must, according to this general, result from "the struggle against the political and economic monopoly of the state."[25]

In other words, the army, the main pillar of the state apparatus resisting the full-fledged implementation of self-managing principles, must struggle against itself. This has confused commanding cadres in the army at all levels. They are expected to maintain strict discipline based on hierarchical principles while respecting the greatest possible freedom for every individual in the army, not only during his off-duty hours but also during his military activities. The existence of this contradiction first became apparent in 1970 at the fourth conference of the YPA party organization. The conference advocated and approved the idea that "a human being is indivisible: a man cannot be free as a communist and not free as a soldier." Military discipline and personal freedom do not conflict, it was claimed. Moreover, "a man is truly disciplined and responsible only to the extent that he is free."[26] After the 1971–1972 purges, however, discipline was re-emphasized.

Army generals have also been involved in the late 1970s discussion about collective leadership. In the debate that followed the report given by Vidoje Žarković at the third plenary session of the Central Committee, Gen. Dane Petkovski, one of Defense Minister Gen. Nikola Ljubičić's deputies, stated that Tito's idea of "collective leadership" had been respected in the YPA:

> Comrade Tito teaches us and demands that responsible officers must, in settling many questions, seek the opinions and proposals of the majority of officers and also of soldiers before adopting decisions. Tito thereby points out to us that such a method makes it incumbent on officers to accept the best proposals, to take responsibility themselves for the decisions adopted, to develop the initiative and creativity of their associates, and to develop their own independence and readiness to accept responsibility for the decisions adopted. This would make it possible in practice for the greatest possible number of people [in the army] to be involved in the collegiate form of work.[27]

This collegiate form of work in the YPA cannot help attracting attention. But having said this, General Petkovski concluded his speech by emphasizing the role of discipline:

> With strict respect for the principle of subordination and single command as the fundamental factor in relations in the YPA, the spirit and meaning of collective work, on which Comrade Tito places such emphasis, is being realized in the army in various forms and ways, without any weakening of the leadership and command.[28]

At this point one should again refer to a report made in June 1970 by Gen. Bozo Šašić in which he criticized those "who are still skeptical" about the idea that soldiers should retain their "personal freedom," "people who cannot conceive of the army in any other way but as total subordination of the lower echelons to the higher ones." But this is precisely what General Petkovski demanded of the soldiers, noncommissioned officers, and officers in the YPA—"strict respect for the principle of subordination and single command."

THE ARMY AND THE PARTY

On 26 December 1978 the sixth regular electoral conference of the LCY organization in the YPA took place in Belgrade. The conference had originally been scheduled for March 1979 since these gatherings are normally held every second year (the preceding two were held in February 1975 and March 1977). It was obvious that Tito's advanced age had prompted party leaders in the army to convene this session three months ahead of schedule. More than 400 delegates participated, but only one senior party and state leader was present: Fadil Hodža, a member of the 24-man Central Committee Presidium and at that time Tito's deputy in the State Presidency. Yugoslavia's most important military leader, General of the Army Nikola Ljubičić, the country's defense minister, did not attend. Instead, the then chief-of-staff, Gen. Stane Potočar (a Slovene), and Gen. Kosta Nadj, president of the war veterans' organization, were mentioned as the most prominent participants in the proceedings.[29]

The main report was submitted by Gen. Džemil Šarac, at the time president of the LCY Committee in the YPA. General Šarac, like the other speakers in the discussion, extolled the strength of the YPA and demanded the strengthening of the defensive potential of the country "to put us in a position to defeat any would-be aggressor, to resist all pressure, and to wage successfully any war imposed upon us."[30]

At the end of August 1978 there were 100,000 party members in the YPA.[31] According to another official source, "over 98 percent of all commanding officers are members of the LCY."[32] (Most YPA officers are party members before attaining officer status.) The sixth conference elected a 90-member committee of the LCY in the YPA, which subsequently elected a 15-member Presidium. A Serb, Gen. Dane Ćuić (until then, head of the security forces in the YPA), was elected president of the committee, and a Montenegrin, Gen. Georgije Jovičić, was elected secretary. Ćuić is one of fifteen officers representing the YPA on the LCY's 166-member Central Committee (Jovičić is not a member). Serbs and Montenegrins now occupy key posts in the party organization in the army. Together with the Serbian Ćuić and the Montenegrin Jovičić, another Serbian general, Milan Daljević, was elected one of the nine executive secretaries on the Central Committee Presidium to represent the party organization in the army.

The percentage of military representatives on postwar LCY central committees has ranged from a low of 3 percent (Fifth and Seventh party congresses) to a high of 10 percent (Tenth Party Congress).[33] Ten percent of those appointed to the Eleventh Central Committee were military delegates, but this figure does not reflect the actual situation. Apart from the fifteen high-ranking officers representing the YPA on the Central Committee, six other army generals (Peko Dapčević, Franjo Herljević, Ivan Kukoč, Kosta Nadj, Dane Petkovski, and Boško Šiljegović) were elected members of the LCY Central Committee by the party organizations in their native republics. In addition, Serbian Gen. Milan Krdžić and Croatian Col. Marijan Vidas were elected to the LCY Statutory Commission and Control Commission, respectively.[34] Hence, 23 high-ranking army officers served on the LCY Central Committee and the two most important commissions, and the actual percentage of army officers on the Central Committee was 14 rather than 10.

The nationality breakdown of the 23 officers representing the YPA (or civilian party organizations) in the LCY Central Committee is eight Serbs, five Croats, two Slovenes, two Montenegrins, two Macedonians, two "Yugoslavs," one Albanian, and one Moslem.

In 1970 the Bosnian theorist Sveto Kovačević saw three chief political deviations in the YPA: a well-meant but naive revolutionary romanticism; an étatistic (that is, Stalinist) mentality; and a "military-professional mentality." He believed that the last deviation, "military technocratism," was the greatest obstacle to the transformation of the army from a "classical army" into one operating on self-management principles.[35] Until the 1971 purges, the party eagerly tried to weaken this techno-bureaucratic attitude in the army by preaching self-management. However, the party also had to contend with a technobureaucratic approach in economic life, which was as dangerous as the army bureaucracy and eventually led to the nationalistic outbursts in Croatia and elsewhere. In May 1970 Prof. Vojislav Stanovčić of Belgrade wrote that "the military bureaucracy is exerting pressure to reach definite political, economic, and ideological solutions that fit military needs; this atmosphere has been created both by these military quarters themselves and by the controlled mass media."[36] Professor Stanovčić saw yet a third bureaucracy between the military bureaucracy and the economic bureaucracy—the party bureaucracy, with its total monopoly of "ideological power." "A struggle is being waged among these three bureaucracies for primacy [in the country] because each of these groups feels itself to be the only real political force," Stanovčić said.

THE COUNTRY'S STRONGEST SUPPORT

Tito's reference to the YPA as his most important and most effective instrument in preserving the unity of the state was not accidental. The YPA is the group most loyal to the Yugoslav state. Regardless of Tito's personal esteem for the party and its organizations throughout Yugoslavia, the army undoubtedly remains the country's—and the party's—strongest support. Since the Ninth LCY Congress (March 1969), the army's influence in Yugoslavia has increased significantly. Particularly since the 1971 purges in Croatia, the army has been extolled as an institution performing "both domestic political and foreign political functions, that is, functions agreeing both with the Marxist conception of the role to be played by military power in the transitional phase and with the needs of our society at its current stage of development."[37] The author of this formula, the theorist Mićo Ćušić, stressed, however, that

> this does not mean that the internal function of the army is its primary function in our society; on the contrary, it is not difficult to prove the opposite. As a result of the development of self-management, socialist relations, and a gradual overcoming of the contradictions inherent in society during the transitional period, the need for the armed forces to fulfill their internal function is increasingly disappearing . . . whereas its external function is becoming its primary function.[38]

Ćušić admitted that the external and internal functions of the Yugoslav army are "in dialectical unity" since the defensive capability of the YPA against any foreign invader is conditioned by domestic developments. General Srećko Manola, who was involved in the 1971 events in Croatia and later disappeared from the Yugoslav military and political scene without being officially purged, said in a lecture to Austrian military experts in Vienna that "when internal tensions within a society have increased beyond a certain point, the capability of resisting dangers from outside diminishes." He added, however, that dangers from outside also "diminish internal conflicts."[39]

For years Yugoslav leaders have pointed to various dangers, coming now from the West, now from the East, especially in connection with the country's internal difficulties. In all such cases, the role of the army, particularly the role it should play on both the military and the political levels, was extolled. Whether Yugoslavia's army generals are ready to play a political role in future developments (especially since Tito's death), they have constantly been hailed as the country's ultimate saviors. Yugoslavia's most prominent jurist, Prof. Jovan Djordjević, said in his major work that "the army always remains one of the important organs of the system, an instrument not only of the country's defense but also of its politics, particularly of the sociopolitical organizations [the party]."[40]

AFTER TITO'S DEATH

In August 1979, nine months before his death, President Tito, in his capacity as the supreme commander of the armed forces, signed a decree appointing Adm. Branko Mamula, a 58-year-old Serb, as Yugoslavia's new chief-of-staff, replacing Slovenian Gen. Stane Potočar,[41] who had reached the retirement age of 60. Following Gen. Dane Ćuić's election as president of the LCY committee in the YPA in December 1978, Admiral Mamula became the second Serb from Croatia to assume a senior position in the YPA.

However, only twelve days after Tito's death on 4 May 1980, General Potočar was returned to active service when a new "Council for Territorial Defense was created in the Federal Secretariat for National Defense" (the defense ministry). His deputy in this "exceptionally significant agency" is Moslem Gen. Rahmia Kadenić, head of the Center of High Military Schools, while a Serb, Col. Mihajlo Čanović, became the council's secretary.[42] The creation of this important new council is the first phase in the centralization of territorial defense, which, according to the Yugoslav Constitution (Article 239), has been strictly decentralized, mainly under the jurisdiction of the autonomous provinces and republics, each of which has its own territorial defense headquarters. True, Article 240 of the Constitution calls the territorial defense forces a part of the armed forces of Yugoslavia, but Articles 16 through 19 of the Law on National Defense provide for their organization as a decentralized institution. For instance, Article 11 (Paragraph 2) of the same law provides that "the responsible authorities of the republics and autonomous provinces and communes shall organize and prepare territorial defense and shall ensure the unity of the organization, preparations, and operations in their territory."[43]

The newly formed council—the members of which "will be representatives of all republican and provincial headquarters of territorial defense, as well as representatives of the defense ministry and a number of
retired comrades [that is, formerly active army officers] who could contribute to the council's successful work"[44]—is certainly not in accordance
with Article 11 of the law. Furthermore, Article 19 provides that "in case
of an immediate danger of war and during a state of war the police force
shall be a part of territorial defense and shall perform its regular tasks,
but it may also be used to carry out the tasks of territorial defense in conformity with the territorial defense plan." This article also provides that
"while carrying out territorial defense tasks the police force shall be sub-
ordinate to the commanding officer of the territorial defense staff or the
officer directing combat operations."[45] All these forces and their com-
manders have thus far been responsible "to the body of the sociopolitical
community that set up the staff" (Article 26 of the Law on National
Defense)—in other words, to the republican and provincial governments.

In Yugoslavia there are three other important defense-related councils: (1) the Council of National Defense (headed by the current chairman
of the Central Committee Presidium, Stevan Doronjski, whose term expired in October 1980), of the eleven members of this council six are
army generals; (2) the Council for the Protection of Constitutional Order
(headed by Dr. Vladimir Bakarić), two of whose eight members are army
generals; and (3) the Council for Civil Defense (headed by Croat Gen.
Ivan Mišković, who was appointed to this post in June 1979). With the
appointment of General Potočar and General Kadenić as heads of the
Council for Territorial Defense, the principle of ethnic distribution
continues to be observed following Tito's death, but mainly in relation to
the Serb, Croat, and Slovene nationalities.

FIVE

The Succession: A Plethora of Candidates

That was an advantage of outliving his time: he appeared timeless, above material things; he seemed beyond good and evil, already glorified by anecdotes and legends, and almost removed from earthly things. The negative aspects of his life had become positive for him; his failures awakened sympathy, his misfortunes made him popular. The endless, long reign also had its good points: one had become accustomed to him, could not imagine how it would be without him, what would happen after him; in him, one knew what one had.

Franz Herre
Kaiser Franz Joseph von Österreich (1978)

The reader might be forgiven for mistaking this description of Kaiser Franz Joseph for that of one of the emperor's sergeant majors at that time—Josip Broz. In World War I the young Broz spilled his Croat-Slovene blood (his father was a Croat, his mother a Slovene) in defense of the Austro-Hungarian monarchy, first against the Serbs, who murdered Archduke Franz Ferdinand in Sarajevo (28 June 1914), and then against the Russians (1915). In Russia he was wounded, captured, and later (in 1917) joined Lenin's Bolshevik October Revolution. Today, more than six decades later, one can only speculate what would have happened to Josip Broz had he been captured in Serbia rather than in Russia. Might he have become an ardent follower of Serbia's (later Yugoslavia's) Karadjordjević dynasty rather than its chief destroyer in World War II? It is an historical fact that in October 1944 Josip Broz, who became world famous under the name of Tito, settled in the Karadjordjević's royal palace in Belgrade. In February 1967, while on an official visit to Vienna, Tito demonstrated his respect for his onetime supreme military commander, Kaiser Franz Joseph, by accepting from Austrian Chancellor Josef Klaus a high military medal he had been awarded by the Hapsburg ruler in 1915 after reports had reached Vienna about the heroic behavior of the then 23-year-old Sergeant Major Josip Broz.[1]

In December 1968, at the age of 76 and with no signs of any serious health troubles, Tito told foreign correspondents in the small Bosnian town of Jajce, well-known as his wartime headquarters, that he had "no time to grow older."[2] Eleven years later, on 25 May 1979, President Tito celebrated his 87th birthday, which was commemorated in Yugoslavia as the "Day of Youth." He seemed to be immortal. In marked contrast, pictures showing his then 68-year-old heir apparent, Edvard Kardelj, during the June 1978 Eleventh LCY Congress in Belgrade revealed that the younger (by eighteen years) man was seriously ill, while the *Stari* ("the Old Man") boasted of his good health. At the end of December 1979 Tito's health began seriously deteriorating. At the beginning of January 1980 doctors failed with a bypass operation to clear an arterial blockage and the subsequent onset of gangrene, which threatened his life. For this reason on 20 January his left leg was amputated. Several days later his health seemed to be improving, but suddenly everything worsened and he was kept alive only by means of "intensive medical measures." Daily bulletins reflected the approaching end, and all over the country people prepared for a period of mourning, full of uncertainty and fear about what might happen after his death. For, as with Kaiser Franz Joseph, Tito's "endless, long reign" had made people "become accustomed to him," afraid even of contemplating what might happen when he was no longer in charge of a country with so many problems and virtually insolvable conflicts. At least "in him, one knew what one had."

But he could not live forever. Despite his good health and dyed hair, his long reign as head of the party and state had to end. And what now? Until recently many Yugoslav state and party officials considered it almost a personal insult when foreigners stubbornly continued to ask what would happen in Yugoslavia after Tito's death. Their ill-humored but ready reply has usually been: "Nothing will happen because everything has been prepared for a smooth succession!" What they meant by smooth succession was that two collective leaderships designed to assume control both of the state and of the party after Tito's death were created: the Presidency of the Socialist Federative Republic of Yugoslavia (popularly known as the State Presidency), and the Presidium of the LCY Central

Committee (popularly called the Party Presidium). Has any member of these two top state and party collective leaderships any realistic chance of emerging as Tito's successor, first as part of a group and eventually as sole leader?

THE STATE PRESIDENCY

The State Presidency, provided for in Articles 313 through 332 of the country's constitution (adopted in February 1974), is composed of nine members: one from each of the six constituent republics and two autonomous provinces, plus Tito in his capacity as president of the SFRY. Before Edvard Kardelj's death the composition of the State Presidency was:

> Josip Broz Tito (president for life)
> Edvard Kardelj (Slovenia)
> Dr. Vladimir Bakarić (Croatia)
> Petar Stambolić (Serbia)
> Cvijetin Mijatović (Bosnia-Herzegovina)
> Lazar Koliševski (Macedonia)
> Vidoje Žarković (Montenegro)
> Stevan Doronjski (Vojvodina)
> Fadil Hodža (Kosovo)

In June 1979 Sergej Kraigher was appointed to replace Kardelj.

At a session in Belgrade on 6 February 1980 the State Presidency decided to change its standing rules (originally announced in 1975 and supplemented in 1977) to include the following seven persons as ex officio members of the State Presidency:

1. Dragoslav Marković, president of Yugoslavia's Assembly (Serb);
2. Veselin Djuranović, Yugoslavia's prime minister (Montenegrin);
3. Stevan Doronjski, in his capacity as chairman of the Presidium. He is already a full member of the State Presidency but will be replaced in October 1980 when his term as chairman of the Presidium expires;
4. Dušan Dragosavac, secretary of the Presidium (a Serb from Croatia);
5. General of the Army Nikola Ljubičić, Yugoslavia's defense minister (Serb);

6. General Franjo Herljević, Yugoslavia's minister for internal
affairs (a Croat from Bosnia);

7. Josip Vrhovec, Yugoslavia's foreign minister (Croat).

These persons, according to Article 22a of the standing rules of the
State Presidency, were to take part in the sessions of the State Presidency
"in case of emergency or any other unforeseeable situation."[3]

The idea of a collective state leadership was born in 1970 when
President Tito, on 21 September of that year, surprised his countrymen
by unexpectedly announcing in Zagreb that a collective state agency
would be created to ensure stability and effective government after he
left the scene.[4] Nine months later, on 27 June 1971, a 23-member State
Presidency (including Tito as its president) was elected in Belgrade on
the basis of the 36th Amendment to the 1963 Yugoslav constitution. It
included three members from each republic and two from each autonomous province, all elected for five-year terms. The 23rd member was
Marshal Tito, acting as president of the State Presidency for life.[5] In
June 1973, the new constitution reduced the size of the State Presidency
from 23 to 9 members. Only two members of the old State Presidency
(Lazar Koliševski of Macedonia and Vidoje Žarković of Montenegro)
were included in the new one.

Article 324 of the constitution provides that "members of the SFRY
Presidency shall be elected for a term of five years" and that "no one may
be elected a member of the SFRY Presidency for more than two
consecutive terms." In February 1979, the Yugoslav media reported that
following Tito's suggestion, the State Presidency's membership for the
next five years (1979–1984) "should remain of the same composition."[6]
This means that Koliševski and Žarković have unconstitutionally entered
their third consecutive terms. Even though Tito himself decided that all
eight members of the State Presidency should remain in their posts,
"preparations have begun in all republics and provinces for the candidacy
and election of members of the State Presidency."[7] In fact, the nominees
suggested by Tito were confirmed by the electorate. Had Tito survived
for the next five years, none of the current members could have constitu-
tionally remained in his post, unless Article 324 of the constitution had
been changed to enable a third consecutive term of five years (for Koliševski and Žarković a fourth term). As we shall see, in 1978 a different
plan had been devised, a plan designed to make the State Presidency a
less significant state agency.

The average age of members of the old State Presidency was 67, the only member under 60 being Vidoje Žarković; in 1979 the average was 66. According to both the constitution (Article 327) and the Operating Procedures of the Presidency (Articles 65 and 66), "the Presidency shall elect a vice-president from among its members" for a period of one year from, in the following order: Macedonia, Bosnia-Herzegovina, Slovenia, Serbia, Croatia, Montenegro, Vojvodina, and Kosovo.[8] For the period May 1979–May 1980 the vice-president (in fact, the "acting president") was the representative from Macedonia, Lazar Koliševski, who automatically became president of the State Presidency following Tito's death, but only for 11 days. On 15 May 1980, when Koliševski's one-year term (355 days as vice-president and 11 days as president) expired, he was replaced as president of the State Presidency by a Serb from Bosnia-Herzegovina, Cvijetin Mijatović, while the Slovene Sergej Kraigher was elected the new vice-president. With Tito's death, the whole chapter of the constitution entitled "The President of the Republic" (Articles 333 through 345) had to be removed, a unique situation in which the constitution was amended not by being changed but by being abrogated. In this way the constitution was reduced from 397 to 384 articles. For a country in which, as a rule, every new constitution or major bill is bulkier than the previous one, this decrease was really exceptional. This reduction was possible because Tito's successor did not assume his dual role as president of the republic and president of the State Presidency. The person elected as the new president of the State Presidency is envisioned by the constitution as combining both offices in one. The sixth paragraph of Article 328 of the constitution reads in full: "With the termination of the office of the President of the Republic, the SFRY Presidency shall exercise all rights and duties vested in it under the present constitution, and the vice-president of the SFRY Presidency shall become president of the SFRY Presidency until the expiry of the term for which he was elected vice-president." It appears quite clear here that "the termination of the office of the President of the Republic" means not only the removal of the provision dealing with this office, but also—with Tito no longer occupying that position—a downgrading of the role of the head of state. This is particularly important in view of the previous intention to choose less prestigious persons to serve on the State Presidency.

In the course of elections to various assemblies throughout Yugoslavia in the first five months of 1978, the Yugoslav media reported a plan intended to create a new type of state presidency, less powerful than the current one. Judging by some of those nominated by individual constituent republics and autonomous provinces, the State Presidency would have become a much less significant collective leadership. Serbia nominated Živan Vasiljević; Bosnia-Herzegovina the Moslem Hamdija Pozderac; Croatia Jakov Blažević; and Kosovo Ali Shukri. No representatives from Slovenia, Macedonia, Montenegro, and Vojvodina were nominated; at least, their names were not published in the press. In May 1978, however, this plan was obviously abandoned (or postponed) because the current composition of the State Presidency was confirmed. No explanation was given for the change of mind.

WITHOUT A NEW TITO

In view of Kardelj's long illness and later death and the consequent lack of a suitable successor to Tito, Tito began propagating the idea of "collective leadership at all levels." The campaign for "collective work" and "collective responsibility" officially began at the seventh session of the Central Committee Presidium, held on 19 October 1978 under Tito's chairmanship. This meeting adopted the standing rules of the Presidium providing among other things for the position of chairman of the Presidium (Chapter 7, Articles 41–43). Although Tito announced his decision to form a collective leadership at the party level in October 1978, Yugoslav leaders and the country's media have, in this connection, focused on Tito's speech at the eighth congress of Yugoslav trade unions in Belgrade on 21 November 1978 in which he also dealt with the new collective organizational structure. The following section of this speech has since been officially cited as heralding the appearance of collectivism:

> It has been generally recognized that during the last few years one-year vice-presidents of the Presidency of the SFRY [the nine-member State Presidency] have been elected. This principle has recently [on 19 October 1978] also been introduced in the Presidium of the LCY Central Committee, to which the Presidium's chairman was also elected for a one-year period. The experience thus far acquired has led to the conclusion that in the next period, it will also be possible to introduce this practice [that is, one-year offices for various presidents and secretaries] in other organs and organizations from the communes to the federation. An exception should be made only in the case of some executive and specialized organs and institutions. But it will be necessary to introduce collective work and demand collective responsibility in them also.[9]

Tito emphasized that this method of collective leadership stemmed from the self-management system and from the system of delegation, from which it should be developed and "gradually implemented." Doubtless Tito was aware that it is much easier to talk about collective leadership than to implement it since not only Yugoslavia's constitution but also many laws must be amended or completely changed in order to accord with this "revolutionary" and "historical" idea of collective work and collective responsibility—as the Yugoslav media have described it. This seems to be the chief reason for Tito's suggestion that collective leadership should be gradually implemented. His hopes can be seen from the following passage of his 21 November speech:

> I have thought much about these problems and am deeply convinced that this manner of work would, to an even greater extent, affirm the collective work designed to contribute to a further democratization of all self-management and political agencies; in this way the appearance of "leader-ism" and other unhealthy ambitions of individuals should be rendered impossible. In short, work would become more efficient while relations among people would become better and more humane.[10]

In discussing the double meaning of collective leadership in Yugoslavia, one immediately thinks of the difficulties that have appeared after Tito's death, both in the party and in the state. There is, however, a third aspect attendant on any charismatic leader, whether in the Soviet Union (after Stalin), China (after Mao), or Yugoslavia (after Tito). A charismatic leader automatically creates thousands of little charismatic leaders, at all levels. In Yugoslavia this is observable not only at the federal, republican, and provincial levels, but also in communes and individual factories. Yugoslavia has thousands of "little Titos" playing the role of unchallenged leader, something that has now been officially branded as "the sin of leaderism."

For all practical purposes, this means that in order to introduce collective work and collective responsibility, one must first remove these little Titos or at least re-educate them to abandon their privileges and authority and, almost overnight, to share their power.

LEADERISM

Charismatic leadership has created a number of deficiencies, which have been publicly denounced in Yugoslavia without, of course, blaming the system as such. For example, a Belgrade daily cited the following "diseases of Yugoslav practice":

> ... separation from the base, various manipulations by informal groups of the interests of the base, and the existence of "irreplaceable" individuals who, because of their functions, have imposed themselves, thus demonstrating their sick careerism and "leaderism," as well as many other defects that have discouraged people from engaging in work of their own free volition; in this way revolutionary zeal has diminished ... and an atmosphere of apathy, a lack of will, and weakness vis-à-vis powerful individuals has been created.[11]

If these weaknesses are not removed by means of collective leadership and collective responsibility at all levels, "passivity, apathy, and dissatisfaction" may negatively influence "ideological-political unity," the paper said. Another issue of the same daily said, in describing the situation nationwide, that "many communities have virtually no new people" because "the same teams have always occupied all leading positions in these communities for the past ten or twenty years, their terms of office being almost unlimited."[12] A similar situation has also existed in enterprises. Branko Mikulić, appointed chairman of the Presidium in 1978, claimed that "the one-year term [for presidents and secretaries] will render a 'death blow' to the bureaucratic-monopolistic ambitions of individuals and groups."[13]

Individuals and informal groups throughout the country are being sharply attacked for leaderism. These people, said another Belgrade analyst, have been unwilling to return to their old jobs after being appointed to leadership positions. They simply do not allow anyone new to assume an important job because "a number of people have become professional politicians, which leads to bureaucratism, 'leaderism,' and careerism." Thus, "deprofessionalizing political life" and introducing real rotation are priorities. According to this analyst,

> in some quarters, for instance, the rule is that people rotate from one office to another. A secretary of the party committee is appointed president of the communal assembly or becomes president of the Socialist Alliance or the trade unions, and vice versa. This has become common: ten "prominent" officials succeed in maintaining themselves at the top as a sort of "cap" with interchangeable functions.[14]

In some cases "an individual has demanded that after his term expires, he be guaranteed a job at the same (if not an even higher) salary than he received while occupying the [party or state] office." Privileges have been so lucrative that few have been ready to leave their posts. "There have very frequently been cases where someone appointed to a [party or state] office received a salary double that of his previous job."[15] While ordinary workers or employees are paid according to the work performed, others earn a great deal simply by occupying an official position. The solution to this unhealthy situation is again the introduction of collective leadership and the deprofessionalization of politics:

> The further development of self-management, the strengthening of collective management, the introduction of one-year offices, and the socialization of cadre policy will undoubtedly contribute to the deprofessionalization of politics and to the return of a person to his previous job after his term expires. However, the suggestion that the payment of appointed officials be changed so that each retains his basic salary [of his previous job] and receives in addition the official allowance for the period he occupies his new position deserves attention.[16]

Can the proposed collective work really solve the existing problems? Tito and his principal colleagues were firmly convinced that this was the only way out of the impasse both in the state and the party. Without doubt, the collective work of the nine-member State Presidency has proved efficient since the one-year vice-presidents have successfully deputized for Tito, though only in ceremonial matters. The situation is different, however, in the 24-member Presidium. The Presidium, not to mention the 166-member Central Committee, is too large for successful collective responsibility. Still, to have a vice-president or chairman for a period of one year is easier at the top than at the base. There have already been suggestions that the concept of one-year presidents be differently implemented in local communities or communes.

Because the constitution prescribes two-year terms for presidents and chairmen of all local communities and self-management "sociopolitical agencies," one-year terms would be unconstitutional. Hence, the chairmen or presidents of various assemblies, conferences, and executive and other agencies should change "from session to session (in alphabetical order)," depending on the governing statutes. Thus, individual members of the organ in question would be responsible "from one session to another."[17] Certainly, in this way any attempt to introduce leaderism would be prevented, but a number of other problems would arise.

As long as Tito was alive, "leaderistic" ambitions were successfully countered by his unquestioned authority. The idea that collective leadership in Yugoslavia will successfully prevent informal groups from continuing with their—thus far—unchallenged rule after Tito's disappearance is a bold one. The real problem remains, however. Existing informal groups are becoming the new collective leaderships; in other words, the practice continues, but the name has changed.

THE PRESIDIUM

The Presidium of the Central Committee was halved to 24 members at the Eleventh LCY Congress in June 1978, and Tito was elected its president for life. In addition to the nine previously mentioned members of the old State Presidency (Tito, the late Kardelj, Bakarić, Stambolić, Mijatović, Žarković, Koliševski, Doronjski, and Hodža), the Congress elected fifteen new members to this supreme party agency. This meant that, with the exception of Tito, who had always been above all other leaders, only eight top officials held offices in both the State Presidency and the Presidium. On 28 June 1979 the sixth plenary session of the LCY Central Committee relieved three members of the Presidium (Kardelj's death in February 1979 had created a fourth vacancy) of their duties and elected four new members to replace them. Lazar Koliševski of Macedonia, Cvijetin Mijatović of Bosnia-Herzegovina, and Vidoje Žarković of Montenegro were relieved of their membership but remained members of the nine-member State Presidency.[18]

Kardelj's post in the State Presidency was taken over by the Slovene Sergej Kraigher, and his place on the Presidium by another Slovene, Andrej Marinc. Koliševski was replaced by his fellow Macedonian Lazar Mojsov; Mijatović (a Serb from Bosnia) by the Bosnian Moslem Hamdija Pozderac; and Žarković by his Montenegrin compatriot Dobroslav Ćulafić. Everyone expected another Slovene to replace Kardelj on the Presidium and, bearing in mind that Mijatović's replacement was announced in February 1979, the replacement of Žarković and Koliševski came as a surprise. All the more so since the remaining four members of the State Presidency (Dr. Vladimir Bakarić of Croatia, Petar Stambolić of Serbia, Stevan Doronjski of Vojvodina, and Fadil Hodža of Kosovo) were not relieved but remained members of both the State Presidency and the Presidium. This means that these four state and party leaders—at least for the time being—rank higher in the party-state hierarchy than the new members. In fact, Article 26 (Section 9) of the new party statutes, adopted at the Eleventh Congress of the LCY, provides that "a member cannot at one and the same time perform executive-political functions in the organs of the League of Communists and in the executive organs of the [state] authorities."[19] Nevertheless, the eight members of the State Presidency (Tito was the ninth) at the time the new party statutes were adopted were all elected members of the Presidium. As we have seen, after the 28 June 1979 session of the Central Committee, only four of them (Bakarić, Stambolić, Hodža, and Doronjski) remained members of both bodies. Another important change in May 1979 was the replacement of Stane Dolanc as secretary of the Presidium by a Serb from Croatia, Dr. Dušan Dragosavac (see below).

The 28 June changes in the top party body partially corrected two essential injustices: joint tenure in state and party functions and an ethnic imbalance. All the newly elected persons, however, are not second-rate but rather third-rate choices. In comparison with Bakarić and Stambolić, for instance, Marinc, Mojsov, Ćulafić, and Pozderac are insignificant political personalities. This is also true when they are compared with their compatriots already on the Presidium, such as Stane Dolanc of Slovenia, Branko Mikulić of Bosnia-Herzegovina, Veselin Djuranović of Montenegro (who is also Yugoslavia's prime minister despite the provision that no duality of party and state functions is allowed), or Aleksandar Grličkov of Macedonia.

It is among these four members of both the State Presidency and the Presidium (Bakarić, Stambolić, Doronjski, and Hodža) that observers look for someone who might emerge as Tito's successor. This is, of course, pure speculation because a possible candidate might also appear from among the remaining four members of the State Presidency or the other nineteen members of the Presidium (despite their not being members of the State Presidency). Among them, General of the Army Nikola Ljubičić is considered the most important.

After Kardelj's death and the 28 June changes, the composition of the Presidium was:

> Tito, LCY president for life
> *For the LC Slovenia:*
> Stane Dolanc
> Andrej Marinc
> Franc Popit, president of the Slovene Central Committee

For the LC Croatia:
Dr. Vladimir Bakarić
Dr. Dušan Dragosavac
Mme. Milka Planinc, president of the Croatian Central Committee

For the LC Serbia:
Petar Stambolić
Miloš Minić
Dr. Tihomir Vlaškalić, president of the Serbian Central Committee

For the LC Bosnia-Herzegovina:
Branko Mikulić
Hamdija Pozderac
Nikola Stojanović, president of the Bosnia-Herzegovina Central Committee

For the LC Macedonia:
Aleksandar Grličkov
Lazar Mojsov
Angel Čemerski, president of the Macedonian Central Committee

For the LC Montenegro:
Veselin Djuranović, prime minister
Dobroslav Ćulafić
Vojo Srzentić, president of the Montenegrin Central Committee

For the LC Vojvodina:
Stevan Doronjski
Dušan Alimpić, president of the Vojvodina Central Committee

For the LC Kosovo:
Fadil Hodža
Mahmut Bakalli, president of the Kosovo Central Committee

For the YPA:
General Nikola Ljubičić, Yugoslavia's defense minister

Each of the six republican parties delegates two representatives to the Presidium; the two provincial parties one each; while the six presidents of the republics' central committees and the two presidents of the provincial committees are ex officio members of the Presidium (Article 81 of the party statutes). The army has only one representative, but this is not (as originally anticipated) the leader of the party organization in the army, Gen. Dane Ćuić, but Yugoslavia's defense minister, General of the Army Nikola Ljubičić.

The ethnic composition of the Presidium was eight Serbs (Stambolić, Minić, Vlaškalić, Dragosavac, Stojanović, Doronjski, Alimpić, and Ljubičić); four Croats (Tito [until his death], Bakarić, Mikulić, and Planinc); three Slovenes (Dolanc, Marinc, and Popit); three Montenegrins (Djuranović, Ćulafić, and Srzentić); three Macedonians (Grličkov, Mojsov, and Čemerski); two Albanians (Hodža and Bakalli); and one Moslem (Pozderac).

It was a great surprise when, at its first session (23 June 1978), the LCY Central Committee did not elect a Moslem to the Presidium. Yugoslavia's 1.7 million Slav Moslems (1.5 million of whom, or 5.8 percent of the country's total population of about 22 million, live in Bosnia-Herzegovina as a separate ethnic group) were—before 28 June 1979—represented neither on the nine-member State Presidency nor on the 24-member Presidium. Almost 87,000 Bosnian Slav Moslems were party members in 1978, that is, 5.5 percent of the LCY's total membership of 1.6 million that year. In comparison, the 400,000 Montenegrins living in the Socialist Republic of Montenegro (or 1.8 percent of Yugoslavia's total population), with only about 60,000 members in the LC Montenegro (or 3.8 percent of the total LCY membership), not only have three full members on the Presidium but one of them (Djuranović) is Yugoslavia's prime minister. Djuranović was appointed prime minister after his predecessor, Džemal Bijedić, died in an air crash in January 1977.

In an interview with the Belgrade television station, Dr. Vladimir Bakarić disagreed with this ethnic distribution of the leading jobs. For instance, "the Serbs have the chairmanship of Yugoslavia's national assembly; the Croats, the chairmanship of Yugoslavia's Trade Union Confederation; Yugoslavia's prime minister is a Montenegrin; etc." In Bakarić's opinion, this situation is improper: "Imagine the situation if we should now change these chairmen every year, so that it might happen that, in one year, all leading positions would be occupied by, say, the Croats."[20] This procedure has to be changed, Bakarić said.

THE LATE HEIR APPARENT

Unquestionably Tito personally approved not only the system of workers' self-management and the socialist market economy, but in addition all aspects of life in the country. Moreover, his foreign policy activities since 1948, especially the policy of nonalignment initiated in 1961, gave Yugoslavia a special image in the international arena, one it did not enjoy before Tito nor is likely to enjoy immediately after him. This is only one of the reasons that Western observers of the Yugoslav political scene have always admired the Yugoslav leader. Even in Eastern Europe, where since 1948 Tito was seldom highly regarded, his grandeur was from time to time publicly acclaimed—admittedly through clenched teeth. In the West Tito's policies were observed through the prism of the East-West conflict, with comparisons being made between Moscow's and Belgrade's communist systems and between their impact on international politics. In the latter case the Yugoslavs are usually rated higher.

It is sometimes claimed that one of Tito's biggest mistakes was his un-usual longevity. Naturally, he could not be blamed on this score, but he could be faulted for failing to resolve the problem of his succession. Only now, after Tito's death, might it become clear that his longevity was a two-edged blade. On the one hand, by retaining full control over the country for so long, Tito preserved the territorial integrity of Yugoslavia and created a more or less artificial unity in the communist party. On the other, the longer he lived, the greater the country's and party's diffi-culties became, making their resolution extremely complex after his death. It is mainly over this point that observers of Yugoslavia differ in dis-cussing its future. Some firmly reject the apocalyptic view of Yugoslavia's destiny after Tito and believe that Yugoslavia, like any other country, will easily survive the disappearance of a dominant national figure.

Most observers find little difficulty in agreeing with this optimistic approach. The question remains, however, of the probable conditions surrounding the transfer of power. As Milovan Djilas once wrote, "the future is known only to the gods and to dogmatists."[21] No one can reasonably speculate either about events in Yugoslavia after Tito's death or about the identity of the country's and the party's next leader. Of the eight members of the State Presidency and of the Party Presidium already mentioned, Kardelj's death left only one who could survive politically without Tito's personal support and on his own authority—the Croat Dr. Vladimir Bakarić. The remaining top officials derived their political power solely from Tito's personal support. His death may lessen or even end their authority. The fates of Georgi Malenkov in the Soviet Union after Stalin's death and, more recently, of certain Chinese leaders following Mao's death are instructive.

Edvard Kardelj's long anticipated death (on 10 February 1979) left a major gap in the country's and party's leadership structure. One of Tito's chief aides since 1937 when Stalin sent Josip Broz to Yugoslavia to assume command of the party, Kardelj himself was in Moscow from 1934 to 1937. In 1941, when the Axis powers attacked and destroyed the kingdom of Yugoslavia, Tito was 49 and Kardelj 31. But Kardelj did not assume his role as Tito's (unofficial) heir apparent until 1966 when Aleksandar Ranković, a powerful Serb Communist who headed the secret police and the organizational structure of the party, was purged for bugging Tito's private apartments. Earlier, Milovan Djilas had been Tito's putative heir apparent, but he was purged in January 1954 for "extreme revisionist views." With Kardelj's and Tito's deaths, not one of the group of four "fascist murderers"—as Moscow branded Tito, Djilas, Ranković, and Kardelj in November 1949—survives.

The usual question posed thus far has been: What after Tito? Let us now ask. What after Kardelj? This does not, of course, nullify the principal question concerning Tito. The problem that arose following Kardelj's death was who was to replace him in his triple role as (1) Yugoslavia's most prominent theorist; (2) Tito's most important adviser; and (3) a native Slovene, an attribute that has played a vital role in the struggle between the Serbs and the Croats.

Kardelj the Theorist

In Djilas's last book, which deals with Yugoslavia during World War II, he said of Kardelj:

> Kardelj is not completely open, though not secretive either, unless he feels threatened in his position and ambitions. On this occasion [October 1943] he was extremely quick and nimble in his thinking, as well as extremely receptive and tolerant in discussions. This was what most attracted me to him. Whenever we were faced with important decisions, it was with Kardelj that I reached agreement most easily. Within the Politburo he was perhaps the only one with whom I could discuss theory—which life constantly stirs up, as it does my mind. Through theorizing, we grew close to each other.[22]

The once famous four—Tito, Ranković, Djilas, and Kardelj—were close to one another, especially after the June 1948 expulsion of Tito and the Yugoslav party from the Cominform. In fact, however, they were divided into two groups. Tito and Ranković were practicians par excellence and cared little for theories. Although Tito's speeches comprised about fifty volumes by 1979, his speeches are interesting not so much for the theories propounded in them (which were usually prepared by Kardelj and his students), but for their expression of his practical policies at home and abroad. Ranković was similar in character. He also was not much concerned with theories, which he left to Djilas and Kardelj, but concentrated rather on action. Tito admired Ranković's practical approach and before June 1966 wanted Ranković to be his heir, although Ranković, a much younger man than Tito, had begun to show signs of impatience with the latter's extreme longevity.

In contrast, Djilas and Kardelj were preeminently theorists. Hence, they enjoyed talking to each other, as Djilas points out, but only as long as the practicians (Tito and Ranković) approved of their theories. In 1953 Djilas went too far, especially after Stalin's death in March 1953 and Moscow's readiness to come to an agreement with the "victorious heretic," Josip Broz Tito. It was Edvard Kardelj (who had originally supported Djilas's revisionist views) who "killed" him theoretically at a Central Committee plenum in January 1954. Kardelj thus remained the most prominent theorist and lawmaker. With Ranković's purge in 1966, Tito removed Kardelj's last possible competitor.

Kardelj the Advisor

Without doubt, Kardelj proved the greatest help to Tito in 1948 when Stalin decided to punish the Yugoslav leader and the Yugoslav party for their heretical behavior. Along with Tito, Kardelj signed the historic letter to Stalin and Molotov in which the now famous words occurred: "No matter how much each of us loves the first country of socialism, the Soviet Union, he should in no case love his own country, which is also building socialism, less."[23] Later, however, other personalities such as Djilas and Ranković also joined the circle of Tito's close advisers. But after Djilas and Ranković were removed, Kardelj was again confirmed as Tito's right hand; he was also his left hand, and, occasionally, even "Tito's head"—producing theories and ideas that the aging leader then propagated in simpler terms, understandable to everyone.

Kardelj the Slovene

Kardelj's ethnic origin was an important factor in his favor due to the permanent quarrel between the Serbs and the Croats. After Ranković's purge in 1966, it seemed almost out of the question that Tito, the son of a Croat father and a Slovene mother, could be replaced by either a Croat or a Serb. The Serbs believe it is enough that a Croat has been ruling the country for more than 30 years and heading the party for over 40. The

Croats, who even under Tito's rule insist that they have been living under a "Greater Serbian dictatorship," would oppose a Serb as Tito's successor, thus making the stabilization of the country impossible.

The solution has been seen in the so-called "Slovene formula"—neither a Serb nor a Croat but a Slovene as Tito's replacement. The Serbs will be happy that a Croat has not come out on top again, while the Croats will be pleased that a Serb has not assumed power over the whole of Yugoslavia. This is why Edvard Kardelj was considered the best solution: a Slovene (although without a firm base in Slovenia), a prominent theorist who was believed (most probably wrongly) to be a man capable of uniting all Yugoslav nationalities.

It is Kardelj's "national" aspect that is now impossible to replace. Yugoslavia has never lacked theorists; every second citizen is one of sorts. It is much easier to find a replacement for Kardelj the theoretician than for Kardelj the Slovene. Stane Dolanc, the next strongest Slovene in Yugoslavia, is incapable of assuming Kardelj's role. For this reason President Tito, on Kardelj's advice, decided to introduce collective leadership at all levels, both in the country and in the party. Since October 1978, four months before Kardelj's death, the Yugoslav media have published numerous articles, speeches, and studies dealing with collective leadership and collective responsibility.

DOLANC AND THE SLOVENE FORMULA

During Kardelj's illness and immediately after his death, Western reports frequently mentioned Stane Dolanc, until 15 May 1979 the secretary of the Presidium, as Tito's most probable successor under the Slovene formula. However, on 15 May 1979, one day before Tito left on a visit to Moscow, the Presidium announced that its new secretary following Dolanc's resignation would be Dr. Dušan Dragosavac, a Serb party official from Croatia. Dolanc remained on the Presidium and was to be given "new tasks."[24] Dolanc's position had begun to weaken five months previously when, on 19 October 1978, the Presidium, meeting in the Montenegrin Adriatic resort of Hercegnovi with Tito in the chair, suddenly decided that the 50-year-old Branko Mikulić, a Croat party official from Bosnia-Herzegovina, should be the first member of the Presidium ever to be authorized to deputize for Tito as party president. The original formulation of the press release issued by Tanjug, the official news agency, said that Mikulić "will execute the functions entrusted to him and chair the Presidium's sessions, as authorized by and in agreement with the LCY president, when the LCY president is prevented from doing so personally." As with Tito's deputies in the State Presidency, Mikulić's tenure was set at one year (in October 1979 he was replaced by Stevan Doronjski).

At first glance the 19 October decision did not seem too significant since Section 2 of Article 82 of the LCY statutes, adopted at the Eleventh Congress, had already provided that "sessions of the Central Committee Presidium of the LCY shall be presided over by the LCY president. When he is prevented from personally presiding over a Presidium session, the LCY president may entrust that duty for each individual session to some other member of the Presidium."[25]

But the party statutes deal with an *individual* session rather than with a one-year term and make no mention of the functions entrusted to Tito's deputy. This may be the reason that the Tanjug release of 19 October omitted any reference to the party statutes. But there was certainly another reason for this omission. Article 84 of the party statutes makes the secretary of the Presidium (at that time Stane Dolanc) the second strongest leader after the LCY president:

> The secretary of the Central Committee Presidium of the LCY, within the framework of his functions, will organize the permanent supervision and implementation of ideological-political attitudes, decisions, and resolutions passed by the Presidium; in agreement with the LCY president he will prepare the sessions of the Presidium; in addition he will coordinate the work of [the nine] executive secretaries of the Presidium and will execute other functions entrusted to him by the Presidium of the LCY Central Committee.[26]

As long as Tito was alive, it was too early to judge whether Stane Dolanc had definitely lost his power. There is no doubt, however, that while secretary of the Presidium, he was compelled to share power—with Branko Mikulić or Mikulić's replacement. Dr. Dragosavac's appointment was for two years, and the standing rules of the Presidium now provide for the alternation of the various nationalities in this post.[27] This was a typical move by Tito, who, since 1966 and especially during Kardelj's long illness, had never allowed any person or group within the state and party apparatus to become too strong. After his experience with Ranković, Tito avoided nominating anyone as his successor, even Kardelj, whom everybody knew to be his choice. However, since Kardelj was seriously ill and was not expected to survive Tito, many Yugoslav and

Western observers had begun to regard Stane Dolanc as Tito's heir apparent.

Dolanc, a very dynamic Slovene known for his exceptional organizational ability, has lacked support among Yugoslav leaders. Only Tito's personal backing made him acceptable. Dolanc became a member of the top party echelons at the end of the 1960s only after Stane Kavčič, at that time Slovenia's prime minister, refused to come to Belgrade as the second Slovene representative in the federation. Following Ranković's purge in 1966, the central party apparatus had been "federalized," giving the party and governmental posts in the republics and autonomous provinces more direct power and greater prestige than the federation's party or state offices. Kavčič did not want to abandon greater power in his native Slovenia for less in Belgrade, especially since the officials representing the republics and provinces in Belgrade were, at that time, regarded as traitors. Dolanc, who had served in both the military and civilian secret police, accepted the offer and moved to Belgrade. His judgment proved correct because the situation in Yugoslavia changed abruptly after the 1971 purges in Croatia and, to an even greater extent, after the Serbian purges in 1972, which Dolanc fully supported. The pendulum of power once more swung to Belgrade.

But Dolanc's chances of becoming a serious candidate for Tito's post as head of the LCY (and later head of state) diminished greatly in 1979. One reason was Dolanc's dubious background. An American journalist revealed that Dolanc, "the executive secretary of the communist party and a ranking figure in the country, belonged as a teenager in Nazi-occupied Slovenia to the Hitlerjugend before he joined the communist party in 1943."[28] Yugoslavia's leaders have firmly and with great disgust rejected any "Spanish solution" after Tito's death, that is, any reconciliation between the wartime opponents. Even dissidents born after 1945 have been proclaimed "fascists," "ustasha" (members of the Croat fascist terrorist organization), or "chetniks" (the noncommunist partisans during World War II). In such a country it is highly improbable that a former Hitlerjugend could emerge as Tito's successor. The veterans of the partisan war (1941–1945), an extremely powerful and conservative group in the country, would consider such a solution an insult to their honor, even if Tito had supported Dolanc's nomination for the succession.

Does this mean that the "Slovene formula" has failed? With Kardelj dead and Dolanc compromised, no other Slovene is capable of assuming power in Yugoslavia with both Serbian and Croat support, as well as with the support of the army, which will undoubtedly play a major role in the succession struggle. Such a man never appeared as long as Tito was alive, for Tito's longevity prevented the solution of the succession problem both in a positive and in a negative sense. Unfortunately Tito was simultaneously the real promoter and guarantor of Yugoslavia's unity and (historically viewed) its demoter and an obstacle to its full realization.

With the failure of the Slovene formula after Kardelj's death and if Tito's legacy is respected by his successors, post-Tito Yugoslavia and the party will be ruled by a collective leadership. The full text of the Presidium's standing rules, adopted on 19 October 1978, regulates "the organization and the method of work" of this supreme body of the party. Based on Article 85 of the party statutes, the Standing Rules contain 69 articles, the first of which stipulates that "the Presidium is a collective, democratic, and political body in which all members have equal rights and responsibilities for its entire work in all areas of its activities."[29]

In addition to Tito, who as LCY president was the unchallenged ruler of the party and had the right to make decisions without asking anyone's approval, the standing rules provide for a new position: "the chairman of the Presidium." This official is authorized "to prepare and convoke the Presidium's sessions following agreement with and authorization by the LCY president and in cooperation with the secretary and other members of the Presidium." The Yugoslav media have hailed the standing rules as a document unique in the entire international communist movement: "Never, thus far, in the history of the international workers' movement has any communist party—as is now being done by the LCY—issued any similar internal document dealing with the rules of behavior for members of the supreme leadership!"[30]

A closer look at the text of the standing rules and the commentaries published in connection with its acceptance reveals that Tito's main aim was to prevent the assumption of full power by a *single* person after his death. Such an attempt might easily lead to serious disturbances in the country, especially in view of the unsatisfactory relations between individual nationalities, particularly between the Serbs and the Croats. In common with almost all Yugoslav bills and regulations, however, the standing rules contain several loopholes that might allow some Presidium leaders to become more equal than others. Paragraph 3 of Article 32 of the standing rules reads in full:

> If, between two sessions of the Presidium, certain decisions are made at a restricted meeting in accordance with the statutory rights of the LCY

president, the chairman, that is, the secretary of the Presidium, will orally or in writing inform the other members of the Presidium at the next session. The information will be included in the session's protocol.[31]

This provision means that not all 24 members of the Presidium must necessarily attend every session. The "statutory rights of the LCY president," however, authorize him to convoke any form of session, which meant that Tito could invite only those Presidium members he wished. Moreover, Article 31 of the standing rules provides that the LCY president and the Presidium as a whole can permit other party and state officials (not members of the Presidium or even of the Central Committee) to participate in the Presidium's sessions.

Yugoslav media especially stress the point that individual members of the Presidium "have equal rights and duties" (Article 34) and "equal rights and responsibilities" for the Presidium's "entire work" (Article 1). Paragraphs 4 and 5 of Article 34 read in full:

> A member of the Presidium will be free to express his critical views at the Presidium's sessions; however, he will not be permitted to disseminate them in the [lower] party organizations or in public without the permission of the Presidium.

> A member of the Presidium will be responsible for the decisions made by and the work of the Presidium as a whole and will be individually responsible for the work delegated to him and for the practical duties allotted to him.[32]

Article 30 of the standing rules provides that "the Presidium can make decisions if at least two-thirds of its members [16] take part in a session." However, "when the problems to be discussed are urgent and the necessary number of members of the Presidium is not available, the session will take place if a majority [13] of all members of the Presidium is present." The decisions passed "will be valid if accepted by the majority of the Presidium's members." Thus, a valid decision can be made by a majority of the minimum quorum, that is, 7 of 13 members. We have seen, however, that Article 32 of the standing rules allows only a few members of the Presidium to make decisions binding on all other members. The standing rules are full of such loopholes.

In interpreting the standing rules, however, the Yugoslav media do not appear to have noticed these loopholes. According to a *NIN* commentary, the most important feature of the Presidium "is that it has been created as a collective political body."

In other words, all members have the same rights and responsibilities for its work. With the exception of the LCY president, all other members of the Presidium are unable to make any decision binding on anyone else without the agreement of the forum [of the Presidium as a whole] to which they were elected [that is, delegated by the republics' central committees].[33]

We have seen, however, that a restricted number of Presidium members (Article 32 of the standing rules) can make binding decisions about which the absent members will be informed after the event.

True, paragraph 3 of Article 30 provides that "if members from a republic or autonomous province do not take part in a Presidium session, they will be informed [about the problem to be discussed] in the fastest possible way and their views on the decisions adopted will be required." In other words, only when all three representatives from a republican party (or two representatives from a provincial party) are prevented from taking part in a Presidium session is their opinion required. Should at least one member from a republican or provincial party be present, he can accept the decision in the name of his colleagues. This is one variation. Another is Article 32 of the standing rules, which permits the LCY President to convoke Presidium meetings "with a restricted number of members" and only later inform other members of the decisions made.

THE COLLECTIVE LEADERSHIP

Besides stipulating that all 23 members of the Presidium (Tito was the 24th, with special rights as long as he was alive) are equal in rights and responsibilities, the standing rules provide for a chairman of the Presidium, who is authorized to deputize for the LCY president for one year. On 19 October 1978, Branko Mikulić, a Croat party official from Sarajevo, was elected to this office. A Serb from Vojvodina, Stevan Doronjski, replaced him in October 1979. The chairman "will preside over the sessions when the president is prevented from" doing so and is also entitled "in cooperation with the Presidium's secretary, with the Presidium's members in charge of individual fields, and with the executive secretaries" to decide the agenda of Presidium meetings. He is also authorized to maintain close contact with the leading officials of individual state agencies, the National Assembly, the trade unions, and SAWPY.

At first glance, one gains the impression that the chairman was the most important figure after Tito. However, Article 43 of the standing rules stipulates that the chairman must be in permanent contact with the secretary of the Presidium and, together with him, "maintain permanent contact with the LCY Presidium." After consultation with other members of the Presidium, particularly with the Presidium's secretary, the chairman is authorized to implement the work programs of both the Central Committee and its Presidium. The chairman and the secretary thus control each other, while both are in turn controlled by other Presidium members.

The executive secretaries (six from the republican parties, two from the provincial parties, and one from the army) are not members of the Presidium but only of the Central Committee. Article 45 of the standing rules provides that the executive secretaries "are responsible for their work directly to the Presidium secretary," again, a provision designed to prevent the secretary from becoming too powerful. All members of the Presidium, all executive secretaries, indeed all other party officials are entitled to "take the initiative" in various discussions and actions. This is especially true of members of the various Presidium commissions, which are allowed to have at most fifteen members each. All commissions are responsible for their work to the Presidium as a whole. In all party bodies provided for by the standing rules, decisions are made "in a democratic way," with the aim "of preventing all tendencies to monopoly" (Article 58).

Article 59 of the standing rules stipulates that the party must exert its influence in all "social organs" by sending delegates to them with the object of defending party interests. The previous article provides that, in this way, the party "will secure for itself all key positions in the social system, thus making it possible for them to remain firmly under the leading influence of socialist forces." Article 61 of the standing rules lays down the following guidelines regarding the behavior of these party delegates:

> The delegates, that is, the representatives of the LCY in the corresponding social organs and bodies, following the policy line prescribed by the LCY, shall be free in voicing and maintaining their views in discussions conducted in those organs, except in the case where the Presidium decides that the [party] delegates are obliged to defend views accepted by the Presidium concerning a specific problem of essential ideological-political and social significance. In such a case they are obliged to defend in these

[nonparty] organs the views maintained by the Presidium and to fight for their implementation.[34]

Article 63 stipulates that the Presidium can organize meetings with members of the Central Committee working in individual republican and provincial organizations as well as in the Assembly of the SFRY "in order to direct their activities in assembly chambers designed to implement the views" of the LCY.

The main purpose of the standing rules of the Presidium is to prevent the acquisition of too much power within the party and the country by any individual. This is easier said than done. As long as Tito was alive, the provisions of the standing rules appeared clear and easy to implement. Even under such conditions, Article 69 allows party leaders to interpret individual articles freely: "The provisions of the standing rules are to be interpreted by the Presidium at its sessions." An article can thus be interpreted one way today and another tomorrow. For example, individual members of the Presidium are "free to voice their critical views" at Presidium sessions, but not in public. A *NIN* commentator explained that

> this formulation was obviously made with the intention of stressing the personal responsibility of every member of this political body. In this context it is appropriate to recall certain occasions in the past when individual party officials made statements and publicly expressed views that contradicted the policy line of the League of Communists of Yugoslavia.[35]

The commentator obviously has in mind not only Milovan Djilas, but also several other top party officials (for instance, Krste Crvenkovski of Macedonia, who in 1970 propagated the idea of an "opposition party"). The ideological struggle must be waged within the Central Committee and its Presidium, and all decisions "will be made by public vote unless the session decides otherwise."

With Tito's death the current standing rules will need to be changed to make a new Tito impossible. Otherwise the new LCY president will automatically assume Tito's role, putting an end to collective leadership. In other words, the real value and significance of the present standing rules will be established only now, after Tito's disappearance.

At a session of the Presidium on 23 October 1979, Tito praised the system of collective leadership within the Yugoslav party, describing it as yet another guarantee of further successes. "There are some people—I also have those abroad in mind—who believe that the introduction of the post of chairman with a one-year term calls the continuity and stability of development into question. This is not true." He added "it is not individuals who ensure the continuity and stability of development but rather the policy line determined by the party and its leaders and the appropriate behavior of the leading cadres."[36] Tito made these comments at the Presidium session at which Doronjski replaced Mikulić.

Five days previously, on 18 October 1979, the eighth plenary session of the LCY Central Committee met in Belgrade under the chairmanship of Branko Mikulić. He revealed in his report that on 30 June 1979 the LCY had 1,855,638 members, of whom 630,904 (34 percent) were "highly skilled, skilled, semiskilled, and nonskilled workers plus peasants."[37] Mikulić said that between 1972 (when the LCY had 1,009,947 members) and the end of 1978 (1,774,624 members), 1,021,411 new members had joined the party. This means that during this period 256,734 lost their party membership. According to previous official statistics, in 1978, the "congress year," 181,320 new members were admitted.[38] Since the party had 1,623,612 members at the end of 1977,[39] this means that 30,308 lost their membership. Mikulić also said that "more than 650,000 party members (or 35 percent) were young people 27 years or younger." There were also 451,000 female members, 24 percent of the total. Mikulić did not disclose, however, the number of white-collar workers in the LCY. Instead he said that if one included engineers, technicians, economists, jurists, and other persons "who directly participate in the production process, as well as young people attending schools that prepare them for productive jobs, then the workers' majority in the party has been achieved."[40] For comparison, at the beginning of 1976 (when the LCY numbered 1,302,843 members) 41.8 percent (or 542,248) were white-collar workers, 28.1 percent (or 366,272) blue-collar workers, 7.5 percent (or 96,139) students and schoolchildren, 5.1 percent (or 65,910) peasants, and 17.0 percent (or 232,274) others.[41]

SIX

Soviet-Yugoslav Relations

One question has always dominated all analyses of relations between Moscow and Belgrade: Will the Russians try to compel Yugoslavia to join the Soviet bloc after Tito's death? Leonid Brezhnev, speaking to a group of workers during a September 1971 visit to Belgrade, disturbed the Yugoslavs by claiming that "to us, as Marxist-Leninists, it is a matter of primary interest that our two countries belong to the same socioeconomic grouping, and this, in the long run, is the important thing."[1]

Tito and his colleagues never tired of insisting that they did not belong to the "same socioeconomic grouping," being fully aware that acceptance of this formulation amounted to virtual approval of any future Soviet intervention in their country's internal affairs. At the same time, however, Yugoslav leaders also attempted to justify certain Soviet moves in other parts of the world, but only where Yugoslav interests were not in danger. After all, the Soviet Union is "the first socialist country" in the world, and "certain corrections" in the attitude of the Soviet leaders would have made it much easier for Yugoslavia to live with the Soviet Union and help it fight for the ultimate victory of socialism and communism. This duality in Tito's approach led to many vacillations in Soviet-Yugoslav relations after Tito's June 1955 reconciliation with Nikita Khrushchev, the 25th anniversary of which was commemorated in Yugoslavia in June 1980.

For years the West has viewed Yugoslavia's struggle against both Soviet and Western influences as its most salient trait. Despite its ideological, political, and economic difficulties (of which the continuous ethnic dissension has been the most troublesome), Yugoslav leaders have succeeded in surviving not only Moscow's anathema between 1948 and 1955, but also all subsequent Soviet attempts to prevent Tito's Yugoslavia from becoming an attractive example for the Soviet bloc countries.

But while Yugoslav leaders have successfully resisted Stalin's, Khrushchev's and Brezhnev's attempts to destroy their self-management system, they have failed to halt a development that has diminished Yugoslavia's influence on the Soviet bloc countries; namely, a decline in the impact of Yugoslav ideology over the past ten or twenty years due to Belgrade's occasionally wavering attitude on Soviet policies. In February 1973, for instance, Tito criticized some Yugoslav journalists for treating the Soviet Union and the United States similarly. "This is not correct," Tito said. "The Soviet Union is a socialist country and is not waging war against anybody." True, he could not agree with the August 1968 invasion of Czechoslovakia, but he still gave Moscow credit for conducting "a course toward reconciliation in the world."[2]

Statements such as these indicate the strength of Yugoslav feeling about the first country of socialism, at least among hard-core communist leaders. However, Tito tended to make such statements at times when Moscow was showing a readiness to help Belgrade financially. The statement quoted above, for instance, came some months after the September 1972 signing of an important agreement providing a huge credit of $1.3 billion to Yugoslavia. Payment was to be in three installments and the first, amounting to $540 million, was the subject of a separate agreement signed on 2 November 1972 in Belgrade.[3] The credits were to be used to buy industrial equipment from the Soviet Union to build and operate 59 industrial plants in Yugoslavia. The first installment, which was to be repaid by the Yugoslavs in goods produced by the Soviet-built industries at a rate of 2 percent interest over a ten to twelve year period, should have been used for the construction and expansion of 38 factories. But from the very beginning, the Yugoslav and Russian approaches to the credit agreement differed. While the Yugoslav media hastened to publish the amount of the Soviet loans, the Soviet press and radio confined themselves to announcing the negotiations and the signing of the agreement, without mentioning any sum. In fact, a Zagreb daily reported at the time that the Yugoslavs had actually requested a $2.0 billion credit, but the Russians had cut the sum to $1.3 billion.[4]

Soon after Tito's February 1973 interview praising Moscow's course toward reconciliation, however, unexpected difficulties arose over the Soviet credits. The Russians had, in fact, begun to exploit Yugoslavia's economic malaise for their own purposes. Drago Buvač, a Yugoslav correspondent in Moscow, advised Yugoslav economists doing business with the Soviet Union to follow three rules: (1) to "depoliticize" their dealings and place them on a strictly economic basis; (2) to prevent Soviet businessmen from "imposing their own rules of the economic game;" and (3) to "abandon their illusion that the Soviet market—which has begun to open itself to the developed countries—can solve the short-term problems of those Yugoslav industries that are not yet included in the world market."[5]

Buvač reported that great difficulties had arisen when Yugoslavia attempted to utilize the first installment of $540 million. He criticized the hastiness of Belgrade authorities in concluding economic agreements with Moscow, saying this was "boomeranging" on the Yugoslavs. He complained that the Soviet Union was trying to sell Yugoslavia products that Yugoslavia did not need and said that the planned economy of the Soviet Union had seriously handicapped Yugoslav utilization of the credits.

In dealing with the Soviet Union, Yugoslav enterprises faced two obstacles. First, to be eligible for a loan, they had to provide considerable funds in Yugoslav dinars to cover the construction costs involved "because in itself the Soviet loan does not cover any of the planned construction." Second, many Yugoslav enterprises "are still hesitating between using Soviet credits or accepting more favorable foreign offers," that is, offers by Western countries. Buvač also revealed that the Russians wanted to incorporate in the Yugoslav-Soviet deal the latest devaluation of the dollar and the nominal revaluation of the ruble. The Yugoslavs refused to agree.[6]

THE PROBLEMS

As this example demonstrates, despite all the reconciliations (invariably followed by new ideological quarrels), the Stalinist past continues to influence Yugoslav-Soviet relations. In the 25 years following the first reconciliation in 1955 (which was almost nullified by the Hungarian revolution of October 1956), the Russians have made numerous attempts to improve relations with Yugoslavia, especially on the state level. Eventually, however, all have ended in failure, mainly because normal interstate relations between communist countries are complicated by the continuing ideological bickering among individual communist parties resulting from the struggle between the Soviet and the Chinese parties.

Yugoslav-Soviet problems since 1948 can largely be reduced to three major issues: (1) the "crisis of capitalism" and its proper treatment (this issue also involves the practical question of relations with Western capitalist governments and the problem of Eurocommunism); (2) the concept of various roads to socialism, recognized by Nikita Khrushchev in the Belgrade Declaration of June 1955 and the Moscow Declaration of June 1956, and later confirmed by Leonid Brezhnev on several occasions; and (3) the meaning of nonalignment and Yugoslavia's role in the nonaligned movement.

Tito visited Moscow in late May 1979 and on his return to Belgrade said that he and Brezhnev had "tried as much as possible to understand each other's points of view on the differences that existed and which, I should say, are logical."[7] *Pravda* regarded these differences as "natural" and "not necessarily an obstacle to our all-round cooperation."[8] Judging from subsequent Yugoslav reporting from Moscow, Tito's main topic in his talks with Brezhnev was the nonaligned movement and its proper interpretation. Tito said that he and Brezhnev had "set out our views on the movement and the policy of nonalignment as an independent, autonomous, and non-bloc factor in international relations." He added that "we stressed that the policy of nonalignment represents for Yugoslavia a basis from which to proceed and a framework for relations with *all* countries" (emphasis added). Tass, in commenting on Tito's words, stated that "*in his opinion*, the exchange of views on the nonaligned movement during the meeting helped reach a more realistic and deeper clarification and understanding of the two countries, of their situation, and of their activities in the world" (emphasis added).[9]

Brezhnev and Tito had last met in August 1977, when the Yugoslav president paid an official visit to Moscow on his way to Beijing. A strict observance of protocol—a sensitive issue among Yugoslav leaders—would have required Brezhnev to visit Belgrade. (The Soviet leader last visited Yugoslavia in November 1976.) Tito's decision to forgo protocol and visit Brezhnev in May 1979 indicated that he regarded these talks as extremely important for relations between the two countries and parties. Shortly before Brezhnev's arrival in Belgrade in November 1976, a Yugoslav newspaper wrote that "where someone comes from is less important that what he wants."[10] What exactly did President Tito want in Moscow?

EUROCOMMUNISM

While defending Eurocommunism against Soviet attacks, Yugoslav Communists have not concealed that their sympathy for the three major West European communist parties (the Italian, French, and Spanish) has been conditional. In an interview with a Zagreb daily, Prof. Stipe Šuvar, Croatia's minister of education and one of the country's younger and more eloquent party theorists, said that "the chances for Eurocommunism are absolutely uncertain because history has not given us enough answers to the question of what it should mean to socialism."[11] This attitude is very close to Moscow's. Another Yugoslav theorist, Zorica Priklmajer-Tomanović, published a booklet entitled *Eurocommunism*, which is generally based on Kardelj's ideas, giving it an official appearance.[12] According to her, the differences of view existing between the LCY and the Eurocommunist parties do not "provoke conflicts and disputes" (p. 67). One of the main differences has been the interpretation of the term dictatorship of the proletariat. According to Kardelj, for Yugoslav Communists "the dictatorship of the proletariat is not a form of political system that hinders the democratization of society." On the contrary, through the system of workers' self-management, which he considers "a special form of the dictatorship of the proletariat," democratization has been implemented.

For Kardelj and Priklmajer-Tomanović, "Eurocommunism is clearly a West European phenomenon, occurring also in some other countries with a similar social structure and international position." Kardelj, in his last book, wrote:

> In fact, "Eurocommunism" is not at all related to the essential idea of communism or to any "regional model" of communism, but rather to a *specific road* toward socialism under the specific contemporary conditions prevailing in Western Europe. Moreover, the policy of "Eurocommunism" is not only a matter of ideology, of social theory and policy—although it also includes these aspects—but also a matter of the practical needs of the West European communist parties, should these parties become a realistic factor in society.[13]

In this context Kardelj said that "it is an obvious truth—referred to by Lenin—that the policy of a communist party working in opposition must not necessarily always coincide with the policy of a party in power, and vice versa."[14] This is "unfortunately forgotten," Kardelj claimed, "which creates the impression that communist parties in individual capitalist countries are dependent on the policy of the socialist countries." According to Kardelj, this view must be firmly rejected.

Yugoslav Communists believe that the Eurocommunists are "very close" to the nonaligned movement, oppose any kind of Stalinism, reject the existence of any "communist center" in Moscow, and wish to separate themselves from all military blocs. On these points, the Yugoslavs believe that the Eurocommunists are their allies, despite the differences between them and the LCY. Nevertheless, Kardelj stressed that "the policy called 'Eurocommunism'—being a specific product of the current conditions prevailing in Western Europe—cannot be accepted as a universal policy line for all countries throughout the world." Moreover, "such a policy line cannot be implemented in a socialist country in which the working class has already acquired power through arms because such a policy would again intensify the conflicts over power; that is, it would open the road to counterrevolution."[15]

In Kardelj's interpretation of Eurocommunism (and consequently in that of all official Yugoslav theorists and analysts), the most important point seems to be that Eurocommunism has a triple role. First, it is a specific road to socialism exclusively for the parties of Western Europe (and other parts of the world where similar conditions prevail) but without any universal value. Second, for Yugoslav Communists Eurocommunism is an extremely valuable ally in the struggle against the communist center in Moscow. In this connection they regularly compare Yugoslavia's expulsion from the Cominform in 1948, which none of the West European parties protested, with some of these same parties' current anti-Moscow attitude. Third, despite extolling some of the Eurocommunist parties' opposition to Moscow, Yugoslav leaders firmly reject the implementation of Eurocommunist ideas either in Yugoslavia or in any Soviet bloc country. The Yugoslav formula seems to be very simple: one should oppose both Moscow's interference in the internal affairs of other parties and any "direct interference" by other parties in the internal affairs of the CPSU. In other words, every communist party and country has the right to march along its own road to socialism.

Priklmajer-Tomanović, like most Yugoslav theorists, dislikes the term "Eurocommunism" (which is claimed to have "many deficiencies"), but she is ready to accept its existence as a fact. Her major criticism is that although the term covers "only Western Europe," it calls itself "Eurocommunism . . . which creates an obvious disharmony between the ex-

tensive area it [theoretically] covers [the whole of Europe] and the limita-
tion of its application [to Western Europe only]." The Yugoslavs are
afraid that in using the term Eurocommunism, the West European
parties "run the risk of homogenizing themselves and placing a common
denominator above all other parties, which—although very close to one
another—have their own specific, historical characteristics and act under
different national conditions." She is also afraid that in calling themselves Eurocommunist, the West European parties "might create a sort
of regional center" (p. 8).

The attitude of Yugoslav party leaders toward the West European
communist parties, especially the Italian and the French ones, has been
none too friendly from the very beginning. Priklmajer-Tomanović re-
calls in her booklet that the founding meeting of the Cominform in late
September 1947 in the Polish town of Szklarska Poreba near Wroclaw
demonstrated that Moscow's real aim was "the control of the European
parties, particularly those that had shown the greatest interest in
autonomy. This control should have been exerted in the name of the
'international interests' of the international communist movement."
Priklmajer-Tomanović writes: "The case of the Italian Communist Party
[PCI] and the French Communist Party [PCF] had remained behind
closed doors at the first meeting of the Cominform; at the second meeting in June 1948 [in Bucharest] the 'case' [of the PCI and PCF] was
publicized in a dramatic way when the conflict between the CPSU and
the Yugoslav Communist Party was revealed" (p. 20).

She fails to mention, however, that Kardelj and Djilas had been
Stalin's mouthpieces in Szklarska Poreba and attacked the PCI and PCF
for their alleged opportunistic views. Vladimir Dedijer wrote in his
biography of Tito that the Russians used the Yugoslavs to attack the PCF
and PCI leaders: "[Andrei] Zhdanov [principal organizer of the Comin-
form] cleverly instructed our representatives Kardelj and Djilas to speak
first in the discussion after the reports delivered by [Jacques] Duclos and
Luigi Longo, the French and the Italian representatives, and to criticize
the policy of their two parties. Kardelj and Djilas needed no persuading,
because the Yugoslav party had deeply critical observations to make on
the work of these two parties during the war and immediately after."[16]
Small wonder, therefore, that the West European communist parties
gladly supported Moscow and Stalin in their anti-Yugoslav campaign
after 1948.

As for current relations between the LCY and the PCF and the PCI, the failure of Georges Marchais in France and Enrico Berlinguer in Italy to achieve their goals by using Eurocommunist propaganda seems to have spoiled some of the LCY's plans. Yet Yugoslavia hailed the 23rd Congress of the PCF (9–13 May 1979) for proclaiming the formula of self-management democratic socialism. Since the "idea of self-management has been included in the party statutes . . . this congress will go down in the history of the PCF as 'the congress of self-management.' "[17] On 2 July 1979 Tito received Marchais on the island of Brioni and expressed full agreement with him on all issues, including "the strengthening of voluntary internationalist cooperation and solidarity based on strict respect for the principles of the equality and sovereign independence of each party."[18] Marchais, in an interview with the Zagreb daily *Vjesnik* on the eve of his arrival in Yugoslavia, said he advocated "self-management socialism of the French color."[19] However, in a book published in 1974, Marchais criticized Yugoslav self-management as leading to "anarchy."[20]

The friendship and cooperation between the LCY and the PCI have been deeper and, for the Yugoslav Communists, of greater importance than their relations with the PCF. The Fifteenth Congress of the PCI (30 March–4 April 1979) was attended by Stane Dolanc, while a number of top PCI leaders (Sergio Segre, Giancarlo Pajetta, Luciano Barca, among others) visited Yugoslavia for meetings with their Yugoslav counterparts. Yugoslav Communists seemed surprised that the Italian Communists were the main losers in Italy's premature national elections (3–4 June 1979)–their vote share decreased by 4 percent. The Yugoslavs blamed the defeat on the PCI's "inconsequence in carrying out reforms as well as their lack of determination for change itself." The second reason, according to the Yugoslavs, was the "failure of the 'experiment' in collaborating with the ruling [noncommunist] majority, because of which the Italian Christian Democrats were the only beneficiaries" of the "historic compromise."[21] This formulation appears to be closer to Moscow's criticism of the PCI than to the earlier, friendlier approach of Yugoslavia.

The significance of this criticism from Belgrade is even more apparent when compared, for instance, with Priklmajer-Tomanović's accusation of interference from Moscow in the internal affairs of other parties. She particularly stressed Moscow's attacks on the Spanish Communist Party and said that "Santiago Carrillo's book [*"Eurocommunism" and the State*[22]] undoubtedly represents a challenge for the CPSU," especially in view of the Spanish leader's ideas about some of Lenin's theories, which he describes as wrong. "An even greater challenge for the Soviet Union" has been Carrillo's "dilemma over the nature of the Soviet system." (Carrillo accepts it as socialist but finds in it certain "unsocialist characteristics.")

Priklmajer-Tomanović says that a party such as the CPSU, "which has always been convinced of its own ideological universality" and whose leaders believe they have achieved a "matured socialism" in their country, must consider Carrillo's ideas hostile, especially since Soviet leaders have never forgiven Carrillo for his condemnation of the 1968 Czechoslovak intervention.

Priklmajer-Tomanović fails to mention that Soviet leaders have yet to forgive Tito for his criticism of the Czechoslovak invasion. Tito, however, forgave them. At a press conference in Slovenia on 4 October 1969 (during Gromyko's visit to Yugoslavia), Tito said that in his talks with the Soviet leader "we arrived at the common conclusion that it is best to forget the past and cooperate on those things that are of common interest to us. Therefore, we are leaving aside the case of Czechoslovakia. It is finished. We no longer wish to raise and dramatize this question, and we have told the Soviet Union so." Although Tito's statement was broadcast by Radio Zagreb on 4 October 1969, no Yugoslav paper published it. In a speech in Zagreb on 10 October 1969 before 300,000 people, Tito repeated that he and Gromyko had decided "to overcome differences from the recent past" but did not mention Czechoslovakia.[23]

VARIOUS ROADS

There is no need to explain once more the historical reasons for Stalin's excommunication of Tito in June 1948 and the reconciliation seven years later (May–June 1955) between Khrushchev and Tito and Moscow's recognition of "various roads to socialism."[24] More useful is a review of some recent developments in Soviet-Yugoslav relations. We should always remember, however, that the impact of the 1948 events can never be completely erased and that many polemics over more recent problems (for instance, the Vietnamese-Cambodian and Vietnamese-Chinese wars, the Soviet invasion of Afghanistan, or Eurocommunism) refer back to these events. The reason for this is simple. On 28 June 1948 Stalin made Yugoslavia and Tito the symbols of resistance against Russian overlordship. The chief accusation against Tito and the CPY contained in the notorious Cominform resolution was that the

Yugoslav party leaders were revising Marxist-Leninist teachings about the party and its duty to retain its leading role. Tito and his colleagues were accused of having "belittled the role of the communist party" and of having "actually dissolved the party in the nonparty People's Front."[25] In 1948 this accusation was clearly nonsense. It is a recognized fact that the Yugoslav leaders did not wish to pursue a separate road to socialism but were forced to do so by Stalin and his East European allies. In other words, the accusation against Tito and his colleagues became true only much later. (The Yugoslavs' problems in making the LCY an omnipotent ruling organization that leads or guides rather than commands are discussed in chapter three.)

In destroying Soviet mythology, Tito and his older colleagues taught younger LCY members that they should not recognize any leading role for the Soviet Union. By this, they meant a commanding role for the Soviet leaders in the world communist movement. They have never rejected a "normal" leading role for the Soviet Union as the strongest socialist country. Consequently, the Soviet leaders are accorded no right to dictate to smaller communist countries but only to protect them and help them achieve socialism by following their own roads. Naturally Yugoslav leaders do not want any protection like the fraternal help accorded Czechoslovakia in 1968. Rather they want full equality between all communist countries and parties, a concept that Moscow has lately accepted in theory but has never been prepared to adopt in practice. For example, an article in the Moscow *Pravda* of 23 May 1980 discussing the "rump" Paris conference of communist parties (28–29 April 1980) warned against any third road.

By insisting on Yugoslavia's sovereign independence and party autonomy, Tito successfully resisted all Soviet attempts to subjugate his country. This stance, however, created internal difficulties. The spirit of independence thus engendered has, in the past 30 years, encouraged younger generations of Yugoslav Communists to become even further estranged from the Soviet Union. Trained to be good Yugoslav Communists without necessarily being loyal to Moscow, these young people have opposed any attempt to subject Yugoslavia to Soviet bloc discipline. But at the same time, they have resented any discipline imposed by their own leaders. The situation thus created is quite unique.

Tito alternated liberal and dogmatic policies, now hounding the domestic pro-Soviet Cominformists, now purging the pro-Western "liberals." However, the result was not the desired strengthening of the moderate course. Instead, the resulting confusion may not become fully

apparent until some time has elapsed after Tito's death. A statement by
Aleksandar Grličkov in June 1978 (published on the day the Eleventh
Congress began) explaining the role of the Yugoslav party best illustrates
this ideological confusion.

> Its role has been to try to find an answer to the question of how in an
> atmosphere of existing different interests under a one-party system, one
> can prevent any possibility of stifling the plurality of interests by the ruling
> party on the one hand and, at the same time, make it impossible to turn it
> into an appendage of the social and political processes in the country . . .
> We have been trying to find ways and means not only of recognizing the
> acceptance of this pluralism but also of beginning a dialogue within the
> party as well as a dialogue between Communists and noncommunists with
> the aim of finding an objective solution acceptable to everyone.[26]

Many of the ideas Grličkov advocates here (which are not exclusively
his own) have since fallen into disfavor, especially the concept of self-
management pluralism, but it is precisely these frequent, campaign-like
changes that seem to most help Soviet activities in Yugoslavia. Neither
the Communists nor the noncommunists know the party's real ideological
position precisely, except for the party's continually repeated claims that
the country must remain independent and that the party must retain its
leading role. Despite the flood of explanatory articles, speeches, and
books, it is extremely difficult to grasp how a country that has not yet
freed itself completely from certain Stalinist attitudes could achieve these
goals, especially now after Tito's death.

A YUGOSLAV VIEW OF THE USSR

The sensitivity and complexity of Yugoslavia's relations with the
Soviet Union have also been elucidated in the 1979 book *Marksizam i
socijalizam* (Marxism and socialism). Its author, Prof. Predrag Vranicki,
former rector of Zagreb University and undoubtedly the country's most
prominent Marxist theorist, deals with Stalinist practices not only in the
Soviet bloc countries but also—to a lesser extent—in Yugoslavia itself.[27]
Vranicki, in the past intimately associated with the journal *Praxis*
(banned in February 1975 because of its revisionist views), refers in his
book "only to the most drastic examples of failures made by Soviet
Marxists, Communists, and ideologists" (p. 233). Some of his assertions
provoked the prompt accusation from Moscow that the book contained

"appeals similar to those of imperialist propaganda, designed to destroy the socialist system."[28] In fact, Professor Vranicki defends Marx and Lenin against Stalin, but in so doing makes little distinction between Stalin's "despotic rule" and the situation under Leonid Brezhnev. For Vranicki the post-Stalin military interventions in Hungary and Czechoslovakia "have not been mere 'incidents' or actions arising accidentally but rather the logical outcome of such [Stalinist] policy and power that have not been overcome by the initial attempts at de-Stalinization" (p. 78).

Even though the anti-Soviet views displayed in Vranicki's book cannot be identified with Tito's and the party's attitude toward the Soviet Union, very little in Vranicki's work would actually meet with official disapproval. It was rather the *timing* of Vranicki's criticism that disturbed LCY leaders and prompted their reaction. In many articles and speeches, Yugoslav leaders and theorists have not hesitated to state their opinion of the Stalinist remnants in Eastern Europe openly. Yet the first official reactions to Vranicki's book were negative, especially after some semi-official reviewers had praised it as a work that "will be approached with full respect by all well-intentioned and genuine Marxist thinkers both in Yugoslavia and throughout the world."[29] A top party weekly sharply rebuked this type of "pathetic apology" and condemned Vranicki's book for not following Marxist theory. The article in question charged that Vranicki did not conceive socialism "as a world process" and did not understand the idea of various roads to socialism. Vranicki was also criticized for placing the phrase socialist country in quotation marks, implying that he had, "in a subjective way," been denying the "socialist character" of many countries. Finally he was accused of a "special kind of dogmatism" of his own.[30]

Why did the Yugoslav authorities, who have always been strict in such cases, allow Vranicki's book to appear? They probably wanted to have it both ways: on the one hand, to allow the book to appear and, on the other, to criticize it for its "serious shortcomings." Generally speaking, Vranicki's analysis seems in full conformity with the official Yugoslav approach to the Soviet Union and other East European countries, especially his criticism of the "present generation of Soviet theorists," who were small children during "Lenin's October 1917" or had only just been born. Thus, Vranicki claims, Yugoslav Marxists "know Marxism as a revolutionary act much better than do the present Eastern ideologists, who did not pass through the fire of armed revolution and who think they can compensate for this by blowing up little balloons with revisionist labels and busily sending them all over the world" (p. 18). In his opinion the Soviet bloc's ruling elites have merely been defending "their privileges, which—contrary to the case with other ruling classes—are not based on private ownership of the means of production and, as a result, reflect only narrow-mindedness." Professor Vranicki believes that the "entire Soviet bureaucracy," because of its social position and its function in the management of the economic and political life of the country, "has become a ruling class." He thinks, nonetheless, that "it would be catastrophic if it were to lose its present power completely." At this point he fully agrees with the ruling group in Yugoslavia that no system other than a socialist one can replace the present bureaucratic rule in the Soviet Union. Nevertheless,

> contradictions, both domestic and foreign, either will have to be resolved by the ruling groups in accordance with the Marxist ideas they have been propagating—regardless of their form—or they will even have to abandon such Marxism and admit in front of the whole revolutionary and progressive world that they have set themselves up as a ruling and exploiting class that has no intention of abdicating without a struggle [p. 99].

Professor Vranicki therefore thinks that predicting "anything about the final consequences of Stalinism" in the Soviet Union and elsewhere is impossible. There are "so many imponderables" that make the situation extremely complex and render it impossible for people to say "whether one or the other eventuality" might occur. Unlike Trotsky and his present-day followers, Vranicki does not believe in the likelihood of a revolution organized by the working class. Without free trade unions, "let alone free political organizations" organized by the working class, no revolution in the Soviet bloc is possible. However, he sees the possibility of an alliance between "undemocratic bureaucratic groups and their military counterparts," which might allow the present rulers to survive for a long time "despite all the possible conflicts that might then ensue within the world's progressive movements, which might strengthen themselves as the ruling class." This might lead the "world communist movement into an unforeseeable situation that would disturb all the existing balances" (p. 100).

Vranicki and top Yugoslav leaders are in full agreement on this point, particularly their common conviction that "within the ruling groups" in the Soviet bloc countries, there are "some forces unwilling to accept obvious contradictions and discord between proclaimed theories and the

real situation." Yugoslav leaders and theorists expect these forces to ra
their voices, especially "against the crisis situation, lags in production,
dissatisfaction among intellectuals, etc." They were, in the past, enthusi-
astic about such attempts, "as in Hungary and Czechoslovakia," where
the situation could have opened "new pages of history." But these
countries were instead "suffocated in the initial phases of their activity by
Eastern bloc intervention" (p. 124). They live in the hope that a new
Nikita Khrushchev will appear and consequently are unwilling to close
the door completely on Moscow.

Professor Vranicki recognizes this. While insisting that the only
resolution for the present impasse in the international communist
movement is the Yugoslav system of workers' self-management, he also
criticizes remaining traces of Stalinism in Yugoslavia. One of the main
features of Yugoslavia's self-management system, according to Vranicki,
has been that it came from above. Hence "many West European Marxists
found it rather strange that such a deep and vital process of thorough
social transformation had been mainly implemented through political
decisions and acts of law" (p. 302). As a result, "the process has been
passing through various difficulties, which would have been less significant in a more developed society." Instead of leading, workers in
Yugoslavia have merely been the "implementers of various ideas"
prescribed from above. The party has principally decided whether
something was "too soon or too late," Vranicki says.

Nevertheless, he believes that, compared with other communist
systems, the Yugoslav system of self-management has many advantages.
He therefore rejects both the capitalist market economy and the Soviet
type of "étatistic-bureaucratic monopoly, planning, and total arbitration."
He anticipates "many new temptations, conflicts, difficulties, and efforts
aimed at achieving a definitive victory of this new and most significant
period in the historical development of man," that is, the victory of the
Yugoslav self-management system (p. 338). Professor Vranicki does not
explicitly say against whom this victory has to be achieved, but no reader
can mistake his implication that Moscow must first be ideologically
defeated before the Yugoslav system can prevail.

NONALIGNMENT

Tito's attitude toward (and his use of) the nonaligned movement was
from the movement's beginning in 1961 conditioned by three main fac-

uggle for Yugoslavia's independence against all at-
major blocs (particularly by the Soviet Union) to join
or the other of the military and economic alliances;
to see all nonaligned countries accept socialism (if
av variety) as the basis for their political and economic
(3)—as a logical consequence of the first two points—
by his efforts to achieve the transition from a bipolar to a bloc-free world,
free of all ideological, economic, and military antagonisms.

Although these three main points have remained theoretically valid
thus far, their implementation is now changing to reflect Yugoslavia's
day-to-day political needs and relations between the two military blocs.
For instance, Tito was closer to the so-called capitalist bloc because of
Western support for his country's struggle for national independence.
The idea that nonaligned states (most of them former Western colonies)
should accept socialism (read communism) as the basis for their general
development, did, however—despite all the ideological quarrels between
Belgrade and Moscow—bring him ideologically closer to the Soviet
bloc. (Or at least this was so until Castro challenged Tito's leadership of
the nonaligned movement.) In the long run this led Tito to accept (and
even to suggest), as a concession to Moscow, that an aligned state like
Cuba be declared not only a nonaligned country but—at the sixth
nonaligned summit in Havana (3–9 September 1979)—even the nominal leader of the nonaligned world, at least until 1982. (Castro expressed
his gratitude by not attending Tito's funeral.)

This was done despite the solemnly proclaimed criteria for determining nonalignment. At the preparatory conference in Cairo (June 1961),
the 25 founding members, under the leadership of Tito, Nehru, and
Nasser, decided on five criteria for membership in the movement: (1) a
country should either pursue a policy of independence based on the
coexistence of states with different political and social systems and on
nonalignment or express the wish to pursue such a policy; (2) a country
should permanently support the movement for national independence;
(3) a country must not be member of a multilateral military pact
concluded in the context of big power confrontation; (4) should a
country sign a bilateral military agreement with a big power or become a
member of a regional defense treaty, such an agreement or treaty must
not have been concluded expressly in the context of big power confrontation; and (5) if a country cedes military bases to a foreign power, this

concession must not have been made in the context of big power confrontation.[31]

These original criteria were somewhat amplified during the preparations for the second nonaligned summit in Cairo (1964) when the countries belonging to the Arab League and the Organization of African Unity were admitted to the nonaligned movement. Later some aligned countries (such as Cuba) were admitted to the movement, forcing the Yugoslavs to rationalize that

> the criteria for nonalignment are not dogmatically formulated. Their vitality is in their dialectical breadth. None of their elements should be approached one-sidedly and statically. Both individually and by their overall effect the elements of the criteria of nonalignment allow for their wide-ranging application, thus precluding the danger of exclusivity, which would be contrary to the spirit of nonalignment.[32]

The Yugoslavs have called this "a more flexible manner" of interpreting the criteria of nonalignment "at the present level of its development."[33] After Belgrade (1961) and Cairo (1964), nonaligned summits took place in Lusaka (1970), Algiers (1973), Colombo (1976), and Havana (1979). At all of them, two different approaches to the interpretation of the criteria for nonalignment conflicted: one insisted on their flexibility and the other demanded their dogmatic application. At the Colombo meeting, a compromise was reached; countries allied with one of the two major blocs were accepted in the capacity of invited guests. Under this status, Romania, the Philippines, and Pakistan were present in Colombo, and the first two in Havana. Nobody, however, questioned the participation of Cuba, although everyone knew that it was a satellite of Moscow. The Yugoslavs defended the participation of countries like Cuba by insisting that the nonaligned movement was sufficiently strong "not to be afraid of the thesis about the Trojan Horse which might penetrate its ranks."[34] They rejected "monolithic, ideological, and exclusive" unity within the nonaligned movement and instead advocated "flexible and dynamic, political and active, open and 'hospitable' " unity.[35] Now that Tito's disappearance from the political scene is a fact, Yugoslav leaders see in a strong nonaligned movement one guarantee of Yugoslavia's independent development after Tito's death. But they regard this as possible only if the nonaligned movement remains genuinely neutral between the two major blocs.

Hence, they have changed their original attitude toward the nonaligned movement as a strictly "socialist domain" because of Vietnam's military intervention (supported by Moscow) in Cambodia and the Soviet Union's invasion of Afghanistan—a nonsocialist and nonaligned country. Since both Vietnam and Cambodia were not only socialist but also nonaligned states, the Yugoslavs amplified somewhat their thesis that nonalignment is a synonym for socialism. "Nonalignment does not automatically bring its member countries social progress and socialist changes," wrote LCY theorist Stanislav Stojanović in a party weekly. "Still less does nonalignment bring any uniform 'model' of socialism, which is one of the main differences between the nonaligned movement and the military-political and ideological blocs. Nonalignment does not prejudice the outcome of social processes in the member countries."[36] Events at the sixth nonaligned summit in Cuba made it obvious that this Yugoslav attitude contrasted sharply with the Cuban approach. The Cubans prefer to regard the nonaligned countries as the "vanguard in the struggle for socialism," especially in the struggle for a "single model," that is, the Soviet one. The September 1979 nonaligned summit demonstrated that although the policy of nonalignment upgraded Yugoslavia's role in international affairs, the movement is polarized, particularly between Yugoslavia and Cuba.

During President Tito's stay in Havana, Yugoslav media spread the slogan: "The nonaligned countries are following Tito's line."[37] This became the official line in a speech by Tito on his return to Belgrade from Cuba. "I want to point out straight away that we are satisfied with the results of the summit," Tito stressed.[38] Despite Moscow's haste to emphasize its own satisfaction with the outcome of the summit, Tito's contentment was, without doubt, sincere. Months before the Havana summit, Tito and his colleagues had been seriously concerned that a deep split might emerge among the participants—thanks to Moscow's activities and Castro's readiness to implement Soviet policy—that would turn the nonaligned movement into an "anti-imperialist" group. During Tito's May 1979 visit to Moscow, one of the main topics of discussion between him and Brezhnev was the nonaligned movement. Judging from events at the Havana summit, the talks were not at all successful from Tito's point of view. This did not prevent each side from repeatedly claiming that its interpretation of nonalignment had prevailed in Havana.

Tito's 4 September speech at the nonaligned summit was considered rather moderate. After months of fierce attacks and counterattacks in defense of what Tito called the "basic orientation" of the nonaligned movement, one might have expected the Yugoslav leader to deliver a more inflammatory speech. But this would not have been prudent. True, Tito had courageously opposed Moscow's domination and hegemony, but at the same time he was careful to avoid any deeper conflict with the Soviet Union in view of the uncertainty over Yugoslavia's fate after his death. In fact, in his Havana speech Tito even made a concession to Moscow: "We have never put all the blocs on the same footing, either with regard to the dates of their formation or with regard to any other characteristics."[39] In other words, for Tito the socialist bloc could not be equated with the capitalist bloc; the former was in principle better because it was socialist.

But he immediately added that "from the very beginning we have therefore raised our voice against bloc policies and foreign domination, against all forms of political and economic hegemony, and for the right of every country to enjoy freedom, independence, and autonomous development." He went on to stress that "we have never accepted the idea of becoming anyone's transmission belt or reserve because this is incompatible with the essence of nonaligned policy."[40]

Needless to say, this concession did not help Tito in Moscow, especially since later in this speech he called for the end of all "undemocratic actions" within the nonaligned movement, a reference to Castro's pro-Soviet manipulations. Tito's insistence that "no foreign military intervention" was acceptable was again aimed at Moscow, referring indirectly to the wars between Vietnam and Cambodia and between China and Vietnam. For him and his fellow Yugoslav leaders, the issue of war between nonaligned countries and foreign armed intervention was vitally important since Tito feared a similar move against Yugoslavia after his death (possibly through Bulgaria).

If President Tito's speech at the Havana summit was moderate, Stane Dolanc's remarks in an interview two days later were not. Asked whether existing differences "have revealed themselves more clearly in Havana than at any other previous conference," Dolanc avoided a direct reply but said that "one bloc in particular has begun to feel that, as a result of the objective situation in which some members of the nonaligned movement find themselves, it could perhaps penetrate the movement." Obviously with Moscow in mind, Dolanc warned against "those who have persuaded certain nonaligned member countries to adopt" radical positions on various questions. In so doing, these unnamed countries have weakened and destroyed "the strength of the nonaligned movement."[41] Both Dolanc and his interviewers criticized Cuba for promoting certain pro-Soviet views, especially over the question of Cambodia's representative in the movement.

THE NONALIGNED DILEMMA

A full-fledged anti-Cuban attack came, however, two weeks after the Havana summit ended. During the conference, Cuban media strongly criticized Yugoslavia's attitude concerning Cambodian representation. The Yugoslavs waited for the results of the 22 September U.N. General Assembly's vote on Cambodian representation before belatedly voicing their anger against Havana's anti-Yugoslav activities. One day after the General Assembly decided in favor of the anti-Vietnamese, anti-Soviet Pol Pot regime, Belgrade approved a counterattack by Tanjug on Prensa Latina, Cuba's official news agency. That same day, in a speech in the Serbian town of Titovo Užice, Tito warned "some people who cannot conceive that the nonaligned movement is no one's mouthpiece."[42] Tanjug explained its delay in replying by saying that the Yugoslavs did not want to disturb the "successful conclusion" of the nonaligned summit. "We did not react to the Prensa Latina commentary, the more so as it failed to receive attention at the moment of the successful conclusion of the conference."[43] If they had reacted belatedly, Tanjug said, it was because *Za rubezhom*, the journal of the Soviet Journalists' Union, "and some papers in the West" had carried or referred to the "attack by Prensa Latina on Tanjug." This, said Tanjug, "obliges us to explain what it was all about, especially because Yugoslav readers have access to the foreign press."[44]

These reasons seem plausible, but the delay was obviously an attempt to conceal a much deeper disagreement between Belgrade and Havana over the proper approach to the nonaligned movement, particularly the problem of Cambodian representation. In the Cuban attack on the Yugoslavs, one of the most important points of disagreement was the question of Cambodian representation at the nonaligned summit. The Cubans considered the "vacant seat" formula that was finally accepted a defeat for which the Yugoslavs were responsible. Tanjug called this Cuban claim "a total distortion" because the Yugoslavs were fighting against "foreign intervention and foreign imposition of a social system and government" rather than trying to resolve "a procedural question of representation at the summit conference." Of course, the defeat suffered by the Russians, Vietnamese, and Cubans over Cambodian representation in the United Nations tremendously strengthened the Yugoslav position and prompted Tito and his colleagues to demonstrate their satisfaction over the victory. In his speech in Titovo Užice, Tito reiterated that "nonalignment is not anyone's reserve or transmission belt . . . It is not and never can be."

Tito's speech was a signal for Yugoslav media to start an anti-Vietnamese campaign stressing that "intervention inspired by allegedly noble and high goals, not even 'in the name of socialism,' must not be recognized" because no foreign country can be allowed "to judge whether one internal regime is 'better' or 'worse' than another."[45] The Yugoslavs gave the following (correct) breakdown of the General Assembly's vote on Cambodian representation: of the 105 U.N. members who participated in the nonaligned summit in Havana, 45 were for Democratic Cambodia (36 full members, 7 observers, and 2 guests), while 22 countries (all full members of the nonaligned movement) were against; 30 members abstained from voting (24 full members, 2 observers, and 4 guests), while 8 members did not take part in the U.N. sessions (5 full members and 3 observers). The nonaligned summit in Havana numbered 116 participants (96 full members, 12 observers, and 8 guests), but some of them—North Korea, Switzerland, the liberation movements—are not U.N. members. Hence, in Yugoslav opinion, the U.N. vote in favor of Democratic Cambodia could "also be seized on as an answer to all those people who—before, during, and after the Havana summit—tried to deprive the nonaligned movement of its non-bloc principles and turn it into their reserve or transmission belt."[46]

Thus far, the Yugoslav approach to nonalignment has been rather confused. On the one hand, Yugoslav Communists have considered the movement a powerful group whose member-countries are striving to achieve socialist goals, which means the nonaligned countries have been Yugoslavia's "natural allies" along the road to socialism. But on the other hand, as Stanislav Stojanović claimed, the Yugoslavs have also raised their voice against "any uniform 'model' of socialism." For them this is "one of the main differences between the nonaligned movement and the military-political and ideological blocs."

This claim does not sound quite plausible. The idea of a uniform model of socialism has been a point of conflict between Belgrade and Moscow rather than between the Yugoslavs and, say, the Americans. Here one can clearly note a serious dilemma confronting the Yugoslavs.

In striving to make the nonaligned movement a powerful group guaranteeing Yugoslavia's independence and sovereignty, they have had to insist on the socialist content of nonaligned ideas. Should they insist too much on socialism, however, they would promote the interests of the Soviet Union, the strongest and most important socialist country in the world. Here we must recall once again Brezhnev's 1971 statement in Belgrade that for the Soviet Union and Yugoslavia "it is a matter of primary interest that our two countries belong to the same socioeconomic grouping," this being "in the long run" the important thing. We have seen, however, that Tito and his colleagues vehemently rejected this idea, fearing that Yugoslav acceptance of this formulation was tantamount to tacit approval of a possible Soviet intervention in Yugoslavia's after Tito's death.

POST-TITO RELATIONS

We are now at the point at which Yugoslavia's attitude toward the nonaligned movement after Tito's death, as well as Soviet activities in Yugoslavia itself, can be discussed in brief. The disagreement over nonalignment has become one of the most important elements in the ideological quarrel between Belgrade and Moscow, and the question arises whether it might continue after Tito's death. President Tito's personal prestige at home and abroad made it possible for Yugoslavia's representatives at various international meetings to maintain their leader's independent line not only on nonalignment but also on Eurocommunism and the various roads to socialism. Will they be able to maintain that line now that Tito is gone? No doubt they will try to, but they are unlikely to be as successful without the protection of their great leader's prestige.

True, Yugoslav media clearly enjoyed the General Assembly vote, when 45 of the 105 nonaligned countries voted against the Soviet Union and Vietnam and only 22 cast votes in their favor. Belgrade sees in this development a great success for Tito, despite 30 abstentions and eight countries that appear not to have voted at all.

The voting in the U.N. General Assembly on 14 January 1980 following the Soviet invasion of Afghanistan was even more disastrous for the Soviet Union. Of the 151 General Assembly members, 104 (most of them nonaligned countries) voted against the Soviet invasion; 18 were in favor; 18 abstained; and 11 (including Romania) were absent. But this anti-Soviet attitude assumed in protest against the invasion of Afghanistan does not necessarily mean the acceptance of a pro-Yugoslav attitude, still less the recognition of Yugoslav leadership. Even the Yugoslavs themselves, though strongly opposed to the Soviet military invasion of Afghanistan, have criticized some of the proposed American measures against the Soviet Union (for instance, economic sanctions or the boycotting of the Olympic Games in Moscow). On the other hand, they happily greeted President Carter's visit to Yugoslavia on 24 June 1980 and the guarantees he repeated for Yugoslavia's sovereignty and independence in view of unspoken but potential Soviet threats.

Milovan Djilas, writing in *Encounter*, seemed very close to the truth when he said: "The countries truly independent of the bloc, undeveloped and for the most part disorganized, have become the most fruitful territory for Soviet penetration."[47] He warned that Yugoslav leaders were deceiving both themselves and others "about the transitory character of these phenomena," especially since Yugoslav leaders—despite Tito's authority in international politics—do not dare involve themselves in an open conflict with the Soviet Union. If they were afraid to do so while Tito was alive, they will be even less inclined to do so now that he is dead. Djilas was of the opinion that Yugoslavia's position, observed "outwardly," has stabilized. "But this only appears to be the case, because both externally and internally Yugoslav policy has deteriorated," Djilas said.[48] He claims that this deterioration has been "more true of foreign policy than it is of domestic policy." But these two elements have always conditioned each other so that the internal deterioration usually led to difficulties in the foreign political field and vice versa. 217795

Moscow has always been very clever in utilizing this development for its own goals. Internally there have been three Yugoslav weak points where Moscow has been very active: the problem of approximately 700,000 Serbs in Croatia; the problem of Kosovo, involving ever increasing conflicts between the Serbs and Albanians; and the problem of Macedonia. In Croatia Soviet agents have been doing their utmost to keep the conflict between the Serbs and the Croats alive. This has never been too difficult. In the early 1970s, before the December 1971 purges in Croatia, some nationalistic Croat émigrés publicly claimed they had been supported by Moscow. Indeed, at least one of the exile extremist nationalist newspapers had a correspondent in Moscow. Dr. Branko Jelić (who died in 1972), a physician and the president of the Croatian National Committee in Munich, created a sensation at the beginning of 1970 by assuming a pro-Soviet line. His newspaper, *Hrvatska država* (The

Croatian State), suddenly began to consider anticommunism unnecessary and announced that its correspondent "Slavko Novak" was to report regularly from Moscow. Novak wrote about a Croatia within the "socialist family"; in an article entitled "Soviet Croatia," *Hrvatska država* advocated Moscow's tutelage.[49] During 1970 similar articles appeared in *Hrvatska država*, which claimed that Moscow had in fact supported the extreme Croat nationalists in Western Europe. Dr. Jelić himself, in a signed leading article in the August/September 1970 issue of *Hrvatska država* entitled "Aspects of the Croatian Policy: The Soviets and the Croats," pointed out that the Croatian people in their struggle for freedom had to consider the facts of the present situation, look for allies, and with their help begin to take action. Other nations might be able to wait patiently for their hour, but not the Croats, for they were in deadly danger. Because the West, including West Germany, had no interest in the freedom and independence of the Croats, the Croats must look for better allies. The United States, Jelić said, was losing prestige and was doing its utmost to disengage itself, politically and militarily, even in the areas vital to it. In contrast, he said, the Soviet Union was present with its dynamic policy everywhere in the world. Hence, the Croat exiles had to change their allegiance. They had to acknowledge that the Russians, from Lenin through Stalin to Brezhnev, had in fact opposed Yugoslavia and favored Croatia's independence from the start. Consequently, Dr. Jelić said, the Croats had no reason to maintain an erroneous anticommunist line and should now ally with the Kremlin.

Of course, not all Croat emigrants have supported Dr. Jelić's pro-Soviet line. Many have vigorously opposed it. For instance, the brother of the late Branko Jelić, Dr. Ivan Jelić (who succeeded him as the leader of the Croatian National Committee in Munich), vigorously protested against those who claim that "the Croats intend to invite the Russians to their country so that, by force of arms, they form a Soviet Croatia."[50] In March 1980 a leading Croat exile monthly carried an illustrated report from Melbourne, Australia, about a meeting of Croats there, describing demonstrators carrying posters with the inscription "Better Soviet Croatia Than American Yugoslavia." The participants in the meeting sent a letter to Leonid Brezhnev saying that "the Croats are not going to defend Yugoslavia against anyone's intervention" because "Yugoslavia should cease to exist in order to preserve peace."[51] In pursuing an allegedly pro-Croat policy designed to create disagreement both between the Croats and Serbs and among the Croats themselves,

Moscow was obviously pursuing a policy similar to Mussolini's. The essence of Soviet policy was to use nationalistic Croat extremism to destroy Yugoslavia and defeat the Serbs; when this was achieved, the Soviets would then support the Serbs against the Croats. Their chief aim has always been the creation of an atmosphere of alarm among the Serbs in Croatia, who have feared a new civil war. This fear has militated against the stabilization of Croatia—and thus of Yugoslavia as a whole.

In the autonomous province of Kosovo, relations between Albanians and Serbs have not been much better. In 1977 of the 1,486,000 inhabitants of Kosovo,[52] 63 percent (or 936,180) were Albanians, 34 percent (or 505,240) Serbs, and 3 percent (or 44,580) others.[53] In the whole of Yugoslavia, there are now an estimated 1.5 million Albanians. In Kosovo, which the Serbs consider the cradle of their national culture and the center of their medieval empire, the two nationalities have been at odds from the very beginning of communist Yugoslavia. Tito's expulsion from the Cominform in 1948 aggravated relations not only between Albania and Yugoslavia but also between Serbs and Albanians in Kosovo. But despite the animosity Tirana has demonstrated against Tito in the past 25 years, Albanian leaders have been rather restrained toward Yugoslavia, especially since their own conflict with Moscow assumed serious proportions in the 1960s. Enver Hoxha and Mehmet Shehu seemed to be aware that anti-Yugoslav activity among the Albanians in Kosovo would only strengthen pro-Moscow elements in Belgrade, an act that might boomerang on Albania.

On 19 January 1980, the Albanian leaders demonstrated their new realpolitik when the party daily *Zeri i popullit* published an editorial entitled "Soviet-Bulgarian Blackmail and Threats Do Not Go in the Balkans." The newspaper condemned the Soviet invasion of Afghanistan and said it was clear that Afghanistan would not be the last victim of "Soviet aggression." It noted that President Tito was ill and said "there are many who say that this situation might incite the Soviet leaders even more to intensify their threatening activity against Yugoslavia." The paper said the Yugoslavs would know how to fight, if need be, with courage and bravery against any attack. It pledged that Albania would never let its territory be used as a stepping stone in any move against Yugoslavia and Greece. Hoxha was quoted as saying at the last party congress in November 1976 that "in the case of any eventual aggression against Yugoslavia by the Soviet Union or some other power the Albanian people will stand by the Yugoslav peoples." *Zeri i popullit* noted that Albania and Yugoslavia had "irreconcilable ideological differences" but that "the Albanians and Yugoslavs will again fight together against their common enemies as they have fought in the past." Yet Djilas, in his *Encounter* article, asked, "Won't Albania, due to its ideological purism, be encouraged to take action on its own behalf rather than hold back?" No doubt, Moscow is keeping the Albanian card in reserve to exert pressure on Yugoslavia in the post-Tito era.

Everything however, will depend on the behavior of Tito's successors toward the Albanians living in Kosovo. Should Kosovo be given the status of a new republic (instead of its current status as an autonomous province), which it has been trying to acquire for years without success, the Kosovo Albanians' general attitude toward the Yugoslav state might improve. In such a case, however, the Serbs' dissatisfaction might increase, thus making them receptive to possible Soviet anti-Albanian propaganda. Thus far, Moscow has done its utmost to avoid anything that might increase anti-Soviet sentiment in Albania, waiting until Hoxha and Shehu disappear from the Albanian political scene.

Finally, the Soviet Union has been encouraging Bulgarian claims to Macedonia. Moscow has played a double-faced role in the dispute between Yugoslavia and Bulgaria over the Macedonian question. The essence of the dispute, which has existed since 1945, is whether, as the Yugoslavs insist, a separate Macedonian nation and Macedonian language exist, or whether, as the Bulgarian Communist Party claims, the Macedonians are in fact Bulgarian. The Soviets have recognized the existence of both an independent Macedonian nationality and a separate Macedonian language (Radio Moscow broadcasts programs in Macedonian). On the other hand, the Russians have never discouraged the Bulgarian leaders' insistence that the Macedonians are Bulgarians.

The Russians did not, of course, invent the conflict. The Yugoslavs and the Bulgarians are themselves responsible for the state of their mutual relations, including the effect of the Macedonian question on them. But Soviet influence has undoubtedly been powerful at times, especially in the past few years. By not helping to resolve the dispute, the Russians have contributed much to instability in that part of the Balkans.

The need for a resolution of this issue is clearly pressing. Without a solution, the Balkans are likely to remain a powder keg that could be used by the Soviet Union to further its Balkan aspirations, especially with Tito gone. Obviously, the matter can be resolved only if Yugoslavia and Bulgaria abandon "greater nationalistic" ideas about the remote past and seek a reasonable solution based on the freely expressed view of the people themselves as to what they consider themselves to be: Macedonians, Serbs, or Bulgarians.

In the absence of such a solution, the Macedonian dispute will remain one of three ethnic trouble spots that could worsen critically now that Tito has passed from the scene. It could happen that with Tito's death, rising tensions over these issues might so complicate Yugoslavia's internal relations that Tito's successors would be forced to devise a new, more direct approach to relations with the Soviet Union. Whether it would be friendlier than the present approach would depend on the militancy with which Bulgarian leaders pursue their anti-Yugoslav activities.

Leonid Brezhnev's attendance at Tito's funeral (in contrast to the absence of Jimmy Carter, Valéry Giscard d'Estaing, and Fidel Castro) was interpreted as a sign of Moscow's goodwill. In addition, a positive appraisal in *Pravda* of the 25th anniversary of the June 1955 Belgrade Declaration (signed by Tito and Nikolai Bulganin as heads of government), recognizing Yugoslavia's separate road to socialism, was regarded as yet another attempt by the Kremlin to avoid—at least for the time being—anything that might produce uneasiness and anxiety among Yugoslavia's nationalities over the possibility of a Soviet invasion along the lines of its intervention in Afghanistan.[54] But while in their commemoration of the Belgrade Declaration the Yugoslavs dealt with it as a strictly country-to-country affair, the Russians tried to involve the two parties also. In none of the Yugoslav commentaries were party relations discussed. Instead, the main principles of the declaration—"respect for sovereignty, independence, integrity, and equality between states in their mutual relations"—were emphasized. A Zagreb paper said that no interference in the domestic affairs of any country would be tolerated, "for any reason whatsoever: economic, political, or ideological."[55] A Belgrade weekly described the declaration as the "Belgrade Magna Carta . . . which unambiguously showed on what principles relations between socialist countries should be based."[56] Most Yugoslav commentators made the point that, during Brezhnev's stay in Belgrade for Tito's funeral, he had said that "the Soviet leadership would like Soviet-Yugoslav relations always to be imbued with an atmosphere of understanding and confidence, cordiality, and absolute equality," and that "joint Yugoslav-Soviet documents today also present a firm basis for close cooperation between the Soviet Union and Yugoslavia."[57]

SEVEN

After Tito

〰〰〰〰〰〰〰〰〰〰〰〰〰〰〰〰〰〰〰〰〰〰〰〰〰〰〰〰〰〰〰〰〰〰〰

The end of the Tito era comes at a time of world disintegration. East-West, North-South controversies erupt almost daily. Conflicts between communist countries are increasing—a development of particular concern to Yugoslav leaders. The bloody armed clashes between Vietnam and Cambodia and Vietnam and China and especially the Soviet invasion of Afghanistan alarm the Yugoslavs, who fear similar actions in the Balkans. To stabilize their country's position internally and externally after Tito's death, Yugoslav leaders need less tension in international relations, particularly in Europe.

Tito's successful 25-year balancing act in foreign policy was made possible by tense relations between the Soviet Union and the United States. For Tito's purpose, which was the preservation of Yugoslavia's independence and its self-managing form of communist dictatorship, it was necessary that relations between Moscow and Washington never be allowed to develop to extremes; that is, the Soviets and the Americans must not get involved in a dangerous confrontation (as in the Eisenhower-Dulles or Kennedy eras), nor should relations become so friendly (as in the Nixon-Kissinger years) that agreement between them over the heads of small states would be possible.

The first alternative would compel Yugoslav leaders to take sides, a development that would inevitably cause ethnic and intraparty strife in Yugoslavia. The second situation might be even more dangerous; Belgrade has always feared division of the world into spheres of influence by the two major blocs, with Yugoslavia eventually crushed between the two millstones. In Tito's opinion, the nonaligned movement was the best (if not the only) safeguard against both these possibilities for an independent and ideologically communist Yugoslavia. Unfortunately, the weakest point of this policy was its basis in Tito's personality cult within Yugoslavia and his great prestige abroad, rather than in the political and economic strength of the system itself.

COLLECTIVE LEADERSHIP

Article 1 of the Yugoslav constitution of February 1974 defines Yugoslavia as

a federal state having the form of a state community of voluntarily united nations and their socialist republics, and of the socialist autonomous provinces of Vojvodina and Kosovo, which are constituent parts of the Socialist Republic of Serbia, based on power and self-management by the working class and all working people; it is at the same time a socialist self-management democratic community of working people and citizens and of nations and nationalities [that is, national minorities] having equal rights.

This article demonstrates the whole complexity of the Yugoslav system: a multinational country calling itself a "self-management democracy," ruled by a one-party dictatorship.

On 4 October 1979, Yugoslavia's State Presidency agreed to submit to the Assembly of the SFRY a proposal to change the constitution adopted in February 1974. The changes, discussion of which began on 31 October 1979 in the Federal Chamber of the Assembly, reflect Tito's idea of a collective leadership and are expected to be accepted in 1981. Article 151, which stipulates the terms of office of various leading officials in national assemblies and governments, has been under particular consideration.[1] It reads in full:

Elected and appointed officials shall be elected or appointed for a term of four years.

Members of the presidencies of the sociopolitical communities and presidents of the executive councils [the governments in the six republics and two provinces] may not be elected for more than two consecutive terms.

Members of executive councils, officials in charge of administrative agencies, and holders of self-management, public, and other functions may be elected or appointed for two consecutive terms and, exceptionally, by a special procedure laid down by the constitution for one more term.

In order to implement the idea of collective leadership, Tito suggested in October 1978 that a one-year term for most elected and appointed leaders should become the rule. In the State Presidency itself, a one-year term for the vice-president (Tito was elected president for life) was the practice even before the new constitution was adopted in February 1974. Article 327 anticipates the post-Tito period when there will be no president for life by providing "for a one-year term."

In a letter to the Assembly of the SFRY, signed by Tito, the State Presidency justified the proposed constitutional changes as a "more consistent implementation of the principle of collective work, decision making, and responsibility in [various] assemblies and other collective organs of the authorities and social self-management."[2] Collective leadership was introduced in the LCY in October 1978, when the position of chairman of the Presidium was established. At a Central Committee plenary session in Belgrade on 18 October 1979, Branko Mikulić, then chairman of the Presidium, further proposed that at the communal, provincial, and republican levels, various party leaders should be elected for shorter periods. For instance, communal party presidents would hold office for a one-year period; secretaries of communal party committees for two years; and executive secretaries would remain in their posts for four years.[3]

THE PARTY AND THE STATE

Since Tito came to power in 1945, the Yugoslavs have changed their constitution four times: in 1946, 1953, 1963, and 1974. The 1946 version was a copy of the Soviet constitution and was replaced by the Constitutional Law in 1953. Ten years later, a new constitution, "the most progressive in the world," was proclaimed. Shortly after its enactment, however, the introduction of changes began. Between 1967 and 1971 no less than 42 amendments were adopted, altering almost everything in the constitution. As a result, a new constitution—again "the most progressive in the world"—was adopted in February 1974. The amendments proposed in 1979, according to Dobroslav Ćulafić, former president of the Assembly's Federal Chamber,[4] are not so much changes as "a process of adjustment of the constitution to the extensive social action designed to implement Comrade Tito's initiative work, decision making, and responsibility."[5] In other words, the frequent constitutional changes are an attempt by Yugoslav leaders to reconcile theory and practice.

The real reason behind the repeated overhauls of the constitution has always been the preservation of party control over the state apparatus. Each new constitution provoked public criticism and discussion, something impossible in other communist countries. For instance, one of the main criticisms leveled against the draft of the 1963 constitution was that it would create a division of authority (as practiced in Western parliamentary systems) rather than unity of authority (as is the rule in the communist countries).[6] Another major criticism was that not only had the term working class been replaced by the expression working people, but also that the draft stated that the withering away of the working class had begun. In fact, this withering away had started as long ago as February 1953 and had originated in the introduction of the workers' self-management system in June 1950 and, theoretically, in the ideas adopted at the Sixth LCY Congress (November 1952), which gave the party an educational rather than a controlling role.

In preparing the 1974 constitution, its authors (of whom Kardelj was the most prominent) attempted to correct the mistakes that they had made ten years before. An ideological compromise was reached: the term working people remained, but the working class (and consequently the party as its vanguard) was given a dominant position. Consequently, Section 4 of the 1974 constitution's preamble begins: "In the Socialist Federative Republic of Yugoslavia all authority shall belong to the *working class*, which is allied with all *working people* in towns and villages" (emphasis added).

Compared with Article 71 of the 1963 constitution, the demarcation between the working class and the working people in Article 88 of the 1974 version is even clearer: "The working class and all working people are the holders of authority and management over other social affairs."

In the State Presidency's letter to the SFRY Assembly, the working class was not mentioned. Instead Tito said that in accordance with the "delegation system, the working people and citizens, through their delegations and delegates, should elect the organs and achieve direct participation in the process of political decision making." He also stressed the validity of the "collective and equal decision making of the working people and their organs, constituted on the basis of the system of delegation." Finally, Tito said that the system of "collective work, decision making, and responsibility" should result in an intensified struggle "against bureaucratic-technocratic usurpation of the self-management rights of the working people and citizens, against leader-ism, careerism, and similar phenomena."[7]

This does not mean, of course, that the party has decided to abandon its leading role and that the term working class will no longer be used. On the contrary, Tito's idea of collective leadership was envisioned as strengthening party control, though not in a dogmatic way. Several years ago Yugoslavia's most prominent constitutional theorist, Prof. Jovan Djordjević of Belgrade, described the role of the party:

> The party may say the truth and is obliged to say it. However, the party only reveals the truth and creates the conditions in which it is formed and expressed; the party elevates the truth to the level of a more general con-sciousness in which one can seek for better and newer truths in sociopo-litical practice, in self-management, in which truth remains a component of that practice, of the people's consciousness.[8]

Professor Djordjević is naturally against any opposition to the com-munist party, but he clearly delineated the party's role when he wrote that "nobody can live and die for another man and nobody can make decisions, manage, plan, and think for him." Edvard Kardelj later adopted this idea in his book on the pluralism of self-management interests. Bearing in mind the personality cult, in both its positive and negative aspects, President Tito said at the 23 October 1979 session of the Presidium that "it is not individuals who ensure the continuity and stability of development but rather the policy line determined by the party and its leaders and by the appropriate behavior of the leading cadres."[9]

The intent of the proposed constitutional changes was to ensure that after Tito, no single individual could usurp power and proclaim himself a "new Tito." Certainly as long as Tito was alive, no such danger existed, but it will be interesting to see whether his successors will again revise the constitution now that he is dead.

DISSIDENCE

One possible reason for the introduction of constitutional changes after Tito's death is the ever increasing opposition to the regime from a number of intellectuals. Mihajlo Mihajlov, after Milovan Djilas one of the best-known dissidents in Yugoslavia, has listed four main groups in the country's dissident movement: (1) many thousand former party members who left or were expelled in 1971 and 1972 (their most prominent voice is Milovan Djilas); (2) Croatian nationalists, not all of whom were party members; (3) the so-called Serbian liberals, who do not display a sharply expressed nationalist character and may even belong to the New Left; and (4) a group of influential professors who were thrown out of Belgrade University in 1975 when *Praxis* was banned (some of them side with Djilas in demanding a system that would allow political parties). There is, however, a fifth group, Mihajlov said, an underground communist party with pro-Soviet and pro-Chinese wings, which has nothing in common with the other four groups although it cooperates with them.[10] During 1979, the Djilas group and the deposed university professors in Belgrade were harassed and threatened, while the Croatian nationalists, the Serbian liberals, and the Cominformists were left more or less in peace. The last group seems to have been completely silenced after its leaders, Col. Vladimir Dapčević, Dr. Mileta Perović, and Prof. Bogdan Jovović, were kidnapped abroad by Yugoslav authorities and imprisoned in Yugoslavia. Both Dapčević (in July 1976) and Perović (in April 1978) were sentenced to twenty years' imprisonment,[11] and Jovović, who reportedly returned to Yugoslavia voluntarily, was acquitted and pardoned in June 1978 after confessing his sins; he was said to have seen the "absurdity" of the anti-Tito struggle.[12] All three lived for many years in the Soviet Union and then suddenly appeared in the West and tried to revive anti-Tito propaganda. Colonial Dapčević was kidnapped by Yugoslav security organs while in Bucharest in August 1975; Dr. Perović was abducted while in Switzerland in July 1977; and Professor Jovović "returned voluntarily" after Perović's kidnapping (he vanished in Paris leaving his personal belongings in his apartment).

The fate of eight Belgrade University professors and lecturers (Mihailo Marković, Svetozar Stojanović, Ljubomir Tadić, Miladin Životić, Mme. Zagorka Pešić-Golubović, Dragoljub Mićunović, Nebojša Popov, and Triva Indjić) has been closely connected with the Zagreb-based *Praxis*. This philosophical journal was founded in 1964 by a group of young Croat philosophers and social theoreticians (among them Prof. Predrag Vranicki), many of whom had actively participated in Tito's partisan units (1941–1945). They supported Tito in his struggle against Stalin and preached a version of Marxism critical not only of Moscow's Stalinism but also of many sensitive social issues in Yugoslavia. One of them, Professor Stojanović of Belgrade, accused his party comrades of carrying out a "Stalinist anti-Stalinism." The *Praxis* group was a rare association comprising both Serbs and Croats. In February 1975 *Praxis* was finally banned, although its Zagreb editors have not been persecuted as much as their Belgrade colleagues.

In January 1974, even before *Praxis* was banned, the Belgrade professors were accused of voluntarily abandoning the party after the June 1968 student riots and of subsequently becoming the "direct instigators and leaders of an extremist opposition and militant group of students who, by their irresponsible activities, have greatly harmed the philosophical faculty in Belgrade."[13] Following these accusations, the dismissal of the dissident professors seemed imminent, particularly after Stane Dolanc, at that time secretary of the Executive Bureau, accused the eight of being anarchists and rightists who only called themselves leftists.[14] On 1 July 1974, however, 150 members of the Scientific Teaching Council voted against the dismissal of the eight professors. Only one member abstained, and no negative votes were recorded.[15] Observers assumed that party members on the council had been instructed to vote in the professors' favor following a meeting in late May 1974 between Tito and the famous West German writer Heinrich Böll, who had advocated liberal treatment of the professors. Soon afterward, their passports, which had been recalled in 1973 and 1974, were returned. (Nebojša Popov had been deprived of his passport since 1968). Without these papers, they had been unable to accept long-term teaching assignments in the West.

When one considers the ages of these professors and lecturers, it is apparent that they were educated and brought up during Tito's struggle with Moscow. In 1948 Stojanović was 17 years old, Životić 18, Mme, Pešić-Golubović 18, Tadić 23, and Marković 25. They can be considered the successful products of Titoism. A comparison of their claims with Tito's remarks of ten or twenty years ago makes it difficult to understand why they were persecuted for their loyalty to Titoism. As with Marx's ideas, Tito's ideas can today be categorized as the ideas of the "young Tito" and those of the "old Tito." The young professors and lecturers remained faithful to the young Tito, and apparently because of this they were persecuted by the old Tito. In 1975 they were suspended from their teaching posts; each has since received 60 percent of his monthly salary, however. In a letter addressed to a West German newspaper, the professors complained about "political discrimination" and about being on a "black list."[16]

The reasons for harassing Milovan Djilas and his friends have been manifold. The Yugoslav leaders' attitude toward Djilas has been dictated not by reason but by emotion, notoriously the worst adviser in politics. Djilas has published a dozen books abroad in which he courageously criticized not only Stalinism but also the communist regime in Yugoslavia. In hundreds of interviews granted to Western newspapers and periodicals, Djilas did not hesitate to stress the depth of his separation from communism. "In Marx and Lenin there is a lot of pure nonsense," he said in an interview, adding that today "nobody really believes in communism . . . When we talk about Communists, we are talking about phantoms. The communism of old is dead. Only the structures it created remain behind."[17]

For these and similar statements made since his break with the party in 1954, Djilas has been criticized and imprisoned. He spent most of the decade between 1956 and 1966 in Yugoslavia's prisons, the same prisons in which the prewar royalist regimes had incarcerated him. "Tito, Kardelj, Ranković, and Djilas" was the refrain of a partisan song. None of the "big four" survived politically: Kardelj died in February 1979, Tito died in May 1980, Ranković was purged in July 1966, and Djilas was removed from all posts in January 1954 and later resigned from the party. He began his dissent by continuing the struggle against the "bureaucratic degeneration" of socialism (the slogan that Tito and his friends inscribed on their banner after the start of the conflict with Stalin in 1948)—even after Tito decided that this struggle had its limits. Over the past 25 years, Djilas has separated himself even more from his old comrades, especially after concluding that the conflict between so-called democratization and one-party rule is irreconcilable. His latest anti-state activity was the publication of a mimeographed periodical called *Časovnik* (Clock) in late September 1979.

Printed in about 500 copies, the periodical consisted mainly of literary works already published abroad but not in Yugoslavia. The main contributors were Mihajlo Mihajlov (a study on Dostoevski), Djilas (two stories already published in English), Prof. Dragoljub Ignjatović, the magazine's nominal editor, and Momčilo Selić. On 15 October Djilas was brought to court with his associates and fined 10,000 dinars (about $530); Ignjatović was given a prison sentence of 30 days, and Selić was reprimanded.[18] (In April 1980, however, Selić was sentenced to seven years' imprisonment.) In a direct attack on Djilas, a Belgrade daily accused

him of having allied himself with "everybody," including extreme nationalists, "trying to organize anti-Yugoslav propaganda." He was said to be
full of hate "for the self-management system and our nonaligned
policy." The end of the article deserves to be quoted in full, for it
obviously implied a last warning to Milovan Djilas and his friends: "We
must repeat that Djilas has been warned several times about his
anti-Yugoslav activities. However, despite all these warnings he has gone
too far. For this reason one must rightly ask the question: How long does
Djilas, with this kind of behavior, intend to go on defying the democratic
patience of our public?"[19]

THE ARMY

But what of developments in Yugoslavia now that Tito is gone? The
official line is that nothing will happen since the country was well prepared
for Tito's departure. As we have seen, however, this is not quite the case.
Nevertheless, one claim of Tito and his colleagues appears to be close to
the truth: Yugoslavia has every chance of surviving as an integral state,
although this depends on a series of preconditions. One of the chief
guarantors of Yugoslavia's national unity has been not the party but the
the army. Doubtless it will also play a decisive role in the post-Tito period
when its task will be not only to resist any foreign attack but also to
preserve Yugoslavia's self-management socialism.

Not all Yugoslav officials are ready to accept this theory. Certainly,
they agree that the YPA plays a decisive role in protecting the country's
national unity and independence, but they firmly reject the suggestion
that it will play a political role after Tito. Replying to certain "reactionary
circles" in the West (which were said to have "falsely speculated" about
Yugoslavia's destiny and future), a Yugoslav theorist characterized the
"prophesies" about the politicization of the YPA as "great nonsense."
This would be impossible, he said, because "Yugoslav society has been
managed by the working class," headed by the LCY. The YPA, a
component of society as a whole, was only an instrument of the working
class, and there was therefore no danger of its assuming a political role.[20]

Neither the sincerity nor the logic of this statement is in doubt;
certainly most Yugoslav Communists share this opinion. They fail to
consider, however, that Yugoslavia cannot be the same country, either
externally or internally, without Tito. If the strength of the YPA is suf-

ficient to resist any attempt from abroad and to prevent any internal disturbance, the solutions to the problems likely to appear after Tito will, in fact, be straightforward. Most observers expect that serious ethnic conflicts will be the principal difficulty for Tito's successors. This problem has, of course, always been acute. Even under Tito its resolution was impossible. But on this point, the army will successfully fulfill its purpose. Yugoslavia's 1979 military exercises were entitled Nothing Must Surprise Us. Yugoslavs have been trained to resist foreign enemies and internal opponents, especially any collaboration between the two. The YPA, in particular, has for decades been trained to face this possibility.

The army has not been prepared, however, to handle one aspect of the country's national policies: the management of Yugoslavia's economy. With Tito dead, two main groups in the Yugoslav leadership will come to the fore. One group, numerically weak, would suggest that Yugoslavia not continue the same grandiose foreign policy it followed during Tito's lifetime. All very loyal Titoists, they would insist that the country should for a time concentrate on internal (especially economic) problems instead of foreign policy. Yugoslavia, they would claim, is an underdeveloped and poor country without the financial means to conduct the sort of foreign policy that Tito managed to do thanks to his enormous prestige both at home and abroad. The continuation of this foreign policy would damage the country internally and consequently harm relations among the different ethnic groups. As a result, Yugoslavs would demand a stricter regime, which might result in increased Soviet influence.

The other, majority group in the leadership would make the opposite claim. According to them, Tito's foreign policy must be continued, even expanded, because this is the only way for the country to survive. Yugoslavia will have to make great material sacrifices to preserve its independence and freedom. Endangered as it is, they would argue, both by the East and by the West, Yugoslavia's leaders must continue both their active opposition to anticommunist opponents domestically and their pursuit of a leading role within the nonaligned movement abroad. The idea that Communists and anticommunists could be reconciled as in Spain after Franco is firmly rejected by the Yugoslav Bolsheviks (the majority group). For years the Yugoslav media have carried innumerable stories about World War II, about partisan struggles, and about exiles allegedly supported by Western reactionary quarters. Even those born after 1945 who have expressed opposition views are automatically branded ustasha or chetniks.

But the effectiveness of this policy line may have ended with Tito's death. Keeping people for decades in a state of permanent war is impossible, especially in Yugoslavia, one million of whose citizens live abroad, mostly in the capitalist West. The army, however, might find it easier to support such a policy against internal and external enemies than to take sides in the likely conflict among Yugoslavia's post-Tito leaders over critical economic issues, with their consequences for domestic and foreign policy. In this situation Tito's collective leadership might easily collapse, leaving the country's destiny in the hands of army generals even less prepared to manage a complicated system than the civilian politicians who preceded them.

The latter were very active both during Tito's long illness and after his death to prevent any single person from becoming a new Tito. The plenary sessions of Yugoslavia's two most important republican central committees—those of the Serbian LC held in Belgrade on 1 March 1980 and of the Croatian LC held in Zagreb on 18 March—revealed that the "real" post-Tito era is to start only after a successful struggle for the "democratization of cadre policy." According to the major reports read at the two plenums, this post-Tito democratization is mainly designed: (1) to have *every* party member included in the work of party organizations; (2) to prevent any *single* person from assuming power at any political and economic level; and (3) to make *collective leaderships* in the communes, provinces, republics, and in the federation, both on the state and party levels, responsible for every decision made. The next important point to emerge from the two plenums is that *personal initiative* should become an inseparable part of the collective decision-making process, with people engaged in that process avoiding any attempt to build up personal power by acting energetic and trying to use that as an indication of their ability. If in the past—and Central Committee members taking part in the discussion could also have said "in the Tito era"—many people enjoyed great reputation and authority not because of their real personal ability but because of the functions they performed, in the post-Tito era, it is people's personal ability that should count more than personal loyalty to any individual leader. The principle of rotation should be strictly implemented to prevent people holding their jobs for eight or more years.[21]

SEVEN AMENDMENTS TO THE CONSTITUTION

Two weeks after Tito's death the Commission of the SFRY Assembly for Constitutional Questions discussed the working text of the Draft Amendments to the Constitution of the SFRY, with the design of strengthening "Tito's idea of collective leadership and collective responsibility."[22] Seven amendments were proposed, by means of which "certain obstacles" in the country's current constitution were to be removed in order to make collective leadership workable at all levels. As anticipated, two different views immediately emerged, especially over the duration of the terms of various functions. The majority of the commission's members were in favor of longer terms, while the minority insisted that Tito's idea should be strictly observed and longer terms should not be permitted. In the opening speech to the Constitutional Commission, the president of the SFRY Assembly, Dragoslav Markovic, said that "we are not going to reappraise our political system as a whole but rather certain aspects of our political practice, so that it harmonizes completely with the system."[23] A Zagreb paper commented, however: "In question are minor constitutional changes, but it should be emphasized that great political changes will be involved."[24]

The *first amendment* deals with the general basis of the collective leadership: its decision-making methods and the responsibility of every member of the collective leadership. The second section of this amendment states that "every member of a collective body shall be personally responsible for his work" and that he "shall be obliged to act in accordance with the principle of the system of delegation and within the given authorization within the duties and rights of the body in question."[25] After ten hours of discussion,[26] the members of the Constitutional Commission agreed that this formulation was "a good basis for the implementation of Comrade Tito's initiative" on collective leadership, even though there were "many new proposals designed to improve the proposed draft text of the amendment."[27]

The *second amendment* regulates the duration of the terms of various offices in general and stipulates that the terms of "nominated and elected officials and other holders of self-management and public offices must not last longer than four years."[28] The "detailed regulation" of this provision should be left to the republics and autonomous provinces. There was deep disagreement over this provision because opponents of the four-year term, who were in a minority in the Constitutional Commission, claimed that the idea of one-year terms was "neither an organizational nor a statutory problem but rather a matter of principle, with deep political significance and sense."[29] In other words, only the acceptance of one-year terms was in full accordance with Tito's idea of collective leadership.

The *third amendment*, providing that the president of the SFRY Assembly be changed every year (and come from a different republic or autonomous provinces), was unanimously accepted. The problem arose whether the president of the Assembly's two chambers (the Federal Chamber with 220 delegates and the Chamber of the Republics and Autonomous Provinces with 88 delegates) should also be elected for a one-year period or for a longer term. The one-year term was proposed.

The *fourth amendment* would change Article 321 of the constitution, which said that "the president of the League of Communists of Yugoslavia is by virtue of his office" a member of the State Presidency. After Tito's death, there is no longer an LCY president, and Article 321 stipulates that "the president of the LCY agency, established in the Statute of the League of Communists of Yugoslavia, shall be by virtue of his office" a member of the State Presidency.

The *fifth amendment* provoked the greatest disagreement in the Constitutional Commission. Three suggestions were made about the election (and re-election) of the country's prime minister and other members of the federal government: (1) the prime minister should be elected (after having been nominated by the State Presidency) for a period of two years (with the right of re-election to another two-year term), while members of the government should be elected for a period of four years (without the right of re-election): (2) the prime minister should be elected from among the members of the government for a two-year period (with the possibility of re-election for a second two-year term), while other members of the government should be elected for a four-year period:[30] and (3) the prime minister should be elected for a single two-year term only, without the right of re-election, while members of the government should be elected for a four-year period.[31]

According to the current regulation (Article 348 of the constitution), the prime minister "shall be elected by the [two] chambers of the SFRY Assembly following a proposal by the State Presidency," while other members of the government are to be proposed by the prime minister–elect "on the basis of the opinion of the Assembly Elections and Appointments Commission." Article 349 of the constitution provides that members of the government and the prime minister "shall be elected for a term of four years" and that no one may be elected prime minister "for more than two consecutive terms," that is, no longer than eight years. As for members of the government, according to Article 349 they may be elected "for two consecutive terms" of four years each, "and exceptionally, by a special procedure laid down by federal statute, for one more [third] term" of four years.[32] As can be seen, both versions of the proposed *fifth amendment* are designed to cut the terms of the prime minister and of members of the government.

The *sixth amendment* changes Article 366 of the constitution, which provided that functionaries in the federal administration were to be appointed for a four-year term, for two consecutive terms, and "exceptionally, by a procedure laid down by federal statute, for one more [that is, a third] term." This third term is now to be completely dropped.

The *seventh amendment* presented no problems; it provides for the term of service of the members of the Constitutional Court of Yugoslavia (eight years) and of its president (one year). The only difference from the current provision is that the presidency rotates every year among the fourteen members of the Constitutional Court (two from each of the six republics and one from each of the two autonomous provinces).

As far as decision making in the eight-member State Presidency after Tito's death is concerned, "every decision must receive at least five of the eight votes," a Belgrade weekly stressed. It emphasized that "a simple majority is valid in all cases except when a different solution is provided in the Operating Procedures" of the State Presidency.[33] A two-thirds majority (six of the eight votes) is required (according to Article 44 of the Operating Procedures) for seven "specific matters": (1) the granting of permission for a law or regulation concerning temporary measures to be enacted; (2) approval of funds for national defense and state security; (3) approval to amend the country's constitution; (4) ratification of a law or other general act of the SFRY Assembly; (5) postponement of enforcement of governmental regulations of general political importance; (6) approval of a nomination for the country's prime minister; and (7) enactment of the Operating Procedures of the State Presidency.[34]

Article 318 of the constitution provides for the dissolution of the competent chamber of the Assembly and the State Presidency if these two agencies do not succeed in resolving a disagreement within six months.

Fifteen days after a newly elected chamber has met, a new State Presidency must be elected.

POST-TITO PARTY LEADERSHIP

Unlike the solution of the post-Tito leadership on the *state* level (the State Presidency), which is provided for in the country's constitution, solving the problem of the post-Tito *party* leadership has encountered serious difficulties. The Party Statutes do not provide for any "collective leadership" similar to the State Presidency. The Presidium of the LCY Central Committee (23 members, without Tito) was considered a "collective leadership" but was never as powerful in the party as the State Presidency was at the state level. This was indirectly admitted by Branko Mikulić in a speech to the Central Committee's Eleventh plenum, held in Belgrade on 12 June 1980, when he said that with the acceptance of the Presidium's Standing Rules in October 1978 the problem of "collective leadership" of the party was only "partially resolved." For a lasting solution, Mikulić said, it would be necessary to convoke an extraordinary party congress, which Tito's successors have been unwilling to do since the regular Twelfth Party Congress is to be held in 1982. Consequently, "the Central Committee and the Presidium," Mikulić said, "should work in accordance with their duties and with the authorization provided for in the Standing Rules of the Party Statutes concerning their work and on the basis of the decisions to be made at today's [12 June 1980] plenum."[35]

These decisions can be summarized in eight points:

1. For the next two years there will no longer be an LCY president, a job that has been held by Tito;

2. Instead, the former chairman of the Presidium (a function introduced in October 1978 in accordance with Article 85 of the Party Statutes, which provides for the acceptance of the Presidium's Standing Rules) was named the president of the Presidium and will be the top party leader for a one-year period (from October to October);

3. The Central Committee shall, however, act as the supreme party agency but will not become a "collective party president"; a "Working Presidium" of five members will have authority during Central Committee sessions;

4. A special commission of the Presidium, composed of ten persons (the president and secretary of the Presidium, plus the six presidents of the republican central committees and the two presidents of the provincial committees) shall make proposals for persons to be elected president and secretary of the Presidium;

5. Other members of the Presidium shall be elected following a proposal by a "special commission" of the Central Committee "on the basis of preliminary consultations" with republican and provincial presidiums;

6. Article 321 of the Yugoslav constitution shall be amended to stipulate who will represent the party in the State Presidency as an ex officio member;

7. The "regional key" shall be strictly observed, so that no two persons from a single republic or autonomous province shall be elected president and secretary of the Presidium; although not specially stressed, it goes without saying that the "nationality key" will also be respected to prevent two Croats, or two Serbs, or any other two members of the same nationality group, from occupying the two most important jobs in the party. This happened in 1979, when a Serb, Dr. Dušan Dragosavac, was elected secretary of the Presidium in May for a two-year period (1979–1981) while another Serb, Stevan Doronjski, was elected president of the Presidium in October for a one-year period;

8. All these "preliminary measures" will be valid until the Twelfth Party Congress in 1982, when definitive solutions will be introduced and a decision made whether the LCY will again have a president, as Tito was, or whether the current "preliminary solutions" will be legalized and the Party Statutes changed.

In the strict sense of the word, the decisions passed on 12 June 1980 were contrary to the valid Party Statutes. Therefore, the period between 1980 and 1982 will be of great significance since the Twelfth Party Congress will either have to approve the "preliminary solutions" or abandon them.

APPENDIX
Who's Who

TITO, Josip Broz (Croat)
Born: 7 May 1892 in Kumrovec (Croatia)[1]
Party Membership: 1920–1980
Titles: President of the Republic; President of the LCY; President of the State Presidency; Supreme Commander of the YPA

Josip Broz Tito, the son of a Croatian father and Slovenian mother, died on 4 May 1980, only a few days before his 88th birthday. During the last years of his life and after his death, the eulogies about Tito surpassed anything that appeared previously about this man, whose fame was, of course, worldwide. Indeed, they read even during his lifetime like obituaries that their authors wished the subject to see. Even though everything said and written about Tito sounds like an affirmation of strength in a country plagued by many weaknesses, the panegyrics have expressed in lofty and often poetic language not only the sincere love Yugoslav Communists cherished for their great leader but also their unconcealed fear about changes after his death.

The seventh of fifteen children, Josip Broz soon came to know poverty, and his life as a locksmith's apprentice quickened his interest in the workers' movement. He subsequently worked as a mechanic both in Vienna and in Germany as an early *Gastarbeiter* (foreign worker) and joined the Social Democratic Party in 1910. In World War I, he was drafted into the Austro-Hungarian army, attained the rank of sergeant major, and was badly wounded and then captured by the Russians on the Galician front. Released from a prisoner-of-war camp after the outbreak of the October Revolution in 1917, he joined the Bolsheviks and fought in the Russian Civil War on Lenin's side. (While in Russia in 1917, he married a local girl named Pelagia who later died; nothing is known of the fate of her Yugoslav successor, Herta. His third (and surviving) wife is the Serb Jovanka, a former major in the partisan army, whom he married after the last war. Mrs. Broz had not been seen in public since June 1977, but reappeared at Tito's funeral.)

Back in Croatia in the early 1920s, Broz actively engaged in political work as a member of the newly created CPY. He was twice detained by the Yugoslav royal police and spent some years in prison (1928–1934) for his political activities. After his release he traveled five times illegally to the Soviet Union where he was groomed for future tasks. In Moscow he was known as "Walter" but also used such other pseudonyms as Ivan Kostanjšek, Slavko Babić, Spiridon Mekas, John Alexander Karlson, Tomanek, Zagorac, and finally Tito.

His career as leader of the Yugoslav Communists began in 1937 after Stalin, whose favorite he was before World War II, purged Milan Gorkić (pseudonym of Josip Čižinski) and appointed Broz secretary of the CPY.

Josip Broz became internationally famous as Marshal Tito during World War II. In 1941 he organized communist-led partisan units to fight both the Axis occupiers of Yugoslavia and his domestic political opponents, whom he accused of (and after the war persecuted for) fraternization with the occupiers. In 1973 it was discovered, however, that Tito had negotiated with the Germans over a cease-fire between the German forces and the partisans. Hitler's foreign minister, Joachim von Ribbentrop, broke off the talks.[2] After the war Tito fulfilled his dream of creating a communist Yugoslavia on the Soviet pattern but soon came into conflict with his powerful protector, Stalin, who was displeased by his protégé's liking for independence.

If Tito's struggle against the Axis powers had made him well known both in Yugoslavia and outside it, his resistance to Stalin made him world famous. Helped by the Western countries and supported by his colleagues, Tito managed to survive. Tito held for life a combination of state, party, and military posts that was unusually powerful, even for a communist leader. His personality cult was so great that Yugoslavia was full of monuments and statues in his honor even in his lifetime. To mark his 85th birthday in 1977 he was awarded Yugoslavia's highest decoration, the Order of National Hero of Yugoslavia, for the third time. His utterances were considered to contain the essence of human wisdom, and millions of copies of his collected speeches have been published.

ALIMPIĆ, Dušan (Serb)
Born: 4 January 1921 in Bačka Palanka (Vojvodina)
Party Membership: 1941–
Current Titles: President of the Vojvodina LC Provincial Committee; ex officio member of the LCY Presidium; member of the LCY Central Committee

Alimpić joined Tito's partisan units in 1941; during the war he was secretary of the district committee of the communist youth organization in his native town and later occupied the same position in Novi Sad, capital of Vojvodina. From 1945 until 1963 he was affiliated with the secret police forces in

Vojvodina and was then appointed secretary of the party committee in Novi Sad. At the Fifth Congress of the Serbian LC in 1965, Alimpić was elected a member of the Serbian Central Committee. In December 1972, after the purge of Mirko Čanadanović, Alimpić was elected president of the Provincial Committee of the Vojvodina LC to replace him in this post. He was reconfirmed in this position at the Tenth (1974) and Eleventh (1978) congresses.

BAKALLI, Mahmut (Albanian)

Born: 19 January 1936 in Djakovica (Kosovo)
Party Membership: 1957–
Current Titles: President of the Provincial Committee of the Kosovo LC; ex officio member of both the LCY Central Committee and of its Presidium

Bakalli was graduated from the High School for Political Science in Belgrade and became a lecturer in sociology at Priština University. Until 1967 Bakalli was chiefly an official of the Youth Federation of Yugoslavia, both in Kosovo and Serbia proper. From 1967 to 1970 he was secretary of the communal party committee in Priština (the capital of Kosovo). In 1968 he became a member of the Central Committee of the Serbian LC and in 1971 was elected president of the Provincial Committee of the Kosovo LC. At the Tenth LCY Congress (1974), Bakalli was elected a member of the LCY Central Committee and ex officio a member of its Presidium; at the Eleventh LCY Congress (1978), he was confirmed in these posts.

BAKARIĆ, Dr. Vladimir (Croat)

Born: 8 March 1912 in the village of Velika Gorica (Croatia)
Party Membership: 1933–
Current Titles: Member of the State Presidency of the SFRY; member of the LCY Central Committee and of its Presidium

Bakarić was graduated from the Zagreb University Law Faculty in 1935 and received his doctoral title in 1937. He is one of Tito's oldest and closest associates. Before the war he was arrested many times for subversive activities. In 1937 he became a member of the Croatian Central Committee's Agitprop Section and in 1940 was elected to the Central Committee of the Croatian party. In 1941 Bakarić joined Tito's partisans and was one of the leading organizers of the liberation struggle in Croatia. Bakarić was the political commissar of the Croatian partisans' headquarters and a member of the Antifascist Council of the National Liberation of Yugoslavia (AFCNLY) and of its Presidium. At the AFCNLY's second session in 1943, Bakarić was elected to the National Committee of Yugoslavia's Liberation, in which he occupied the position of deputy commissar for foreign affairs.

Bakarić, the son of a judge and a lawyer himself, began his actual rise to power in 1944 when he was elected secretary of the Croatian party, a post he occupied until 1966 when he was elected president of the Croatian Central Committee. He was prime minister of Croatia from 1945 until the constitutional reorganization in 1953, when he was appointed president of the Croatian National Assembly (1953–1963). In 1963 Bakarić became a member of the Yugoslav government; he was also a member of all postwar national assemblies, both in Yugoslavia and Croatia. He has been a member of the LCY Central Committee since 1948 and of the Presidium since 1966. At the Tenth (1974) and the Eleventh (1978) LCY congresses, he was confirmed in these posts. Between 1952 and 1966 Bakarić was a member of the party's Executive Committee and later of the Presidium. At the Ninth LCY Congress (1969), he was included in the LCY Executive Bureau. In January 1972, when the Executive Bureau was reorganized as an eight-man body, Bakarić relinquished his place but remained influential as a party theorist. He was Tito's principal supporter in the drive against the so-called Croatian nationalists. Bakarić has the title of National Hero of Yugoslavia.

ČEMERSKI, Angel (Macedonian)
Born: 31 March 1923 in Kavadarci (Macedonia)
Party Membership: 1942–
Current Titles: President of the Central Committee of the Macedonian LC; ex officio member of the LCY Central Committee and of its Presidium

Čemerski was graduated from the Economics Faculty of Skopje University. He joined Tito's partisans in 1941 and was politically active during the Bulgarian occupation of Macedonia. In 1941 he became secretary of the Youth Federation of Yugoslavia's (SKOJ) Bureau in the Economics School in the Macedonian town of Bitolj; between 1942 and 1943 he was a member of the SKOJ's local committee in Kavadarci. Only in 1943 did he become a soldier of the Tikveš Partisan Detachment; in the Second Macedonian Shock Brigade, he was the head of the Propaganda Department. In the Macedonian towns of Štip, Strumica, and Bitolj, Čemerski was a secretary in the area and district committees of the SKOJ. After the war Čemerski was a member of party organizations in Skopje, the capital of Macedonia, and of the Macedonian government; he was, in turn, deputy minister for industry and mining, chairman of the Committee for Communal Affairs, vice-president of the Economic Council, director general of the food and tobacco industry, and director of the Macedonian Institute for Economic Planning. Čemerski was first elected a member of the Macedonian LC Central Committee in May 1959 at the Third Congress; he was confirmed in this post in March 1965 at the Fourth Congress and in November 1968 at the Fifth Congress, which also elected him secretary of the Executive Committee. In March

1969 Čemerski was appointed to his present post as president of the Macedonian LC following the major reconstruction of the LCY leadership and of the federal and regional administration. At the Sixth Congress of the Macedonian LC (April 1974), Čemerski was re-elected president of the Macedonian Central Committee. At the Tenth LCY Congress (1974), he was elected a member of the LCY Central Committee and ex officio of its Presidium; the Eleventh LCY Congress (1978) confirmed him in these posts.

ĆULAFIĆ, Dobroslav (Montenegrin)
Born: 16 January 1926 in Andrijevica (Montenegro)
Party Membership: 1944–
Current Titles: Member of the LCY Central Committee and of its Presidium

Ćulafić was graduated from the Belgrade University Law Faculty and from the High Party School in Belgrade. He joined Tito's partisans in 1943. After the war Ćulafić became a member of the Belgrade University party committee and president of the Central Committee of the People's Youth of Montenegro. He was also secretary of the Main Committee of the Socialist Alliance of the Working People of Montenegro, and secretary of the Ivangrad Communal Committee in Montenegro. At the Eighth LCY Congress (1964), Ćulafić was elected a member of the LCY Central Committee. In 1966 he took office as a Central Committee secretary of the Montenegrin LC, and at the Ninth LCY Congress (1969), he was elected to the Presidium and worked on the Commission for the Development of the LCY. In October 1969 he was elected president of the Socialist Alliance of the Working People of Montenegro. He was appointed deputy prime minister of Yugoslavia in May 1974 and was made chairman of the Commission for Sociopolitical and Organizational Questions. At the Tenth LCY Congress (1974), he was elected to the LCY Central Committee but became a member of the Presidium only in February 1975. He was not confirmed in this position at the Eleventh LCY Congress (1978), but in June 1979 he replaced Vidoje Žarković as Montenegrin LC representative on the LCY Presidium. Between May 1978 and November 1979 Ćulafić was president of the Assembly's Federal Chamber.

DJURANOVIĆ, Veselin (Montenegrin)
Born: 17 May 1925 in the village of Martinići (Montenegro)
Party Membership: 1944–
Current Titles: SFRY Prime Minister; member of the LCY Central Committee and of its Presidium

Djuranović interrupted his secondary education in 1941 and joined Tito's partisans, but was caught and detained by the Italians until 1943. During the war he was one of the Youth Federation's (SKOJ) district-level leaders in

Montenegro. After the war he occupied various posts in youth and party organizations, was secretary of the party's district committees in Danilovgrad and Titograd, a member of the Montenegrin Central Committee's Agitprop Department, a member of the SKOJ's provincial committee, and president of the People's Youth of Montenegro. Between 1953 and 1958 Djuranović worked with the press and radio; he became director of "Radio Titograd" and editor of the newspaper *Pobjeda* (Victory). From 1958 to 1962 he headed the Commission for Ideological Work of the LCY Central Committee. In 1966 he was elected secretary of the Montenegrin LC Executive Committee. At the Fifth Congress of the Montenegrin LC (December 1968), Djuranović was elected president of the Central Committee of the Montenegrin LC. He was confirmed in this post at the Sixth Congress (April 1974). At the Tenth LCY Congress (1974) Djuranović was elected a member of the LCY Central Committee and an ex officio member of its Presidium. In March 1977, following SFRY Prime Minister Džemal Bijedić's death in an airplane accident, Djuranović was elected prime minister. At the Eleventh LCY Congress (1978), he was confirmed in his Central Committee and Presidium posts.

DOLANC, Stane (Slovene)
Born: 16 February 1925 in Hrastnik (Slovenia)
Party Membership: 1944–
Current Titles: Member of the LCY Central Committee and of its Presidium

Dolanc joined Tito's partisan units in Slovenia only in 1944, when he also joined the party. During the war he lived in the part of Slovenia that was annexed by the Third Reich, and he reportedly belonged to the Hitler Youth. He was graduated from the Law Faculty of Ljubljana University. He served in the military Counterintelligence Service (KOS) until 1960 and later occupied several party posts in Ljubljana, where he also was director of the High School for Political Science. At the Fifth (March 1965) and Sixth (December 1968) congresses of the Slovenian LC, he was elected a member of the Central Committee and of its Executive Committee, respectively.

At the Ninth LCY Congress (1969), Dolanc was elected both a member of the newly formed 52-member Presidium and of the fifteen-member Executive Bureau headed by Tito. In January 1972 (at the Second LCY Conference), Dolanc was elected secretary of the new eight-member Executive Bureau. At the Tenth (1974) and the Eleventh (1978) LCY congresses, he was confirmed in this post (the title was changed to secretary of the Presidium). In May 1979 Dolanc resigned as the Presidium's secretary but remained a member of the Presidium. He was replaced by Dr. Dušan Dragosavac.

DOLNIČAR, Ivan (Slovene)
Born: 31 July 1921 in Sujica (Slovenia)
Party Membership: 1941–
Current Title: Secretary-General of the State Presidency

General Dolničar joined Tito's partisan units in 1941 and was, in turn, company, battalion, brigade, and divisional political commissar. After the war he was graduated from the High School for Political Science in Belgrade and the High Air Force Academy and completed a military operations course at the YPA Military Academy. He was successively political commissar of a division, deputy commander of an air force corps, and chief-of-staff of the Air Force Academy. He was elected a member of the LCY Presidium at the Eighth (1964) and Ninth (1969) LCY congresses but not at the two subsequent congresses. In the later 1960s General Dolničar was appointed deputy defense minister and since 1972 has been secretary of the State Presidency's Council for National Defense and Tito's deputy in the latter's capacity as supreme military commander of the Yugoslav armed forces. In June 1978 General Dolničar was appointed to the eleven-member Yugoslav National Defense Council. Several days later, Tito made him secretary-general of the State Presidency, the nine-member supreme state collective leadership.

DORONJSKI, Stevan (Serb)
Born: 26 September 1919 in Krčedin (Vojvodina)
Party Membership: 1939–
Current Titles: Member of the State Presidency of the SFRY; member of the
LCY Central Committee and of its Presidium

Doronjski studied before the war at the Veterinary Faculty of Belgrade University. He was active as a communist official in his native province of Vojvodina and was also secretary of the party organization in his faculty. He joined Tito's partisans in 1941 and organized a resistance movement in his native district. In September 1941 he was appointed political commissar of the Danubian Partisan Unit. Later he became a district party secretary. In 1945 Doronjski became organizational secretary of the Central Committee of the Youth Federation of Yugoslavia, and later secretary of the Provincial Committee of the Vojvodina LC and also president of the Provincial Assembly of Vojvodina. Doronjski has also been a member of the Executive Committee of the Serbian LC, secretary of the Belgrade Municipal Party Committee, and secretary of the Serbian LC Executive Committee. At the Sixth (1952) through Eleventh (1978) LCY congresses, he was elected a member of the Central Committee and of the Presidium. In March 1969 Doronjski was appointed a member of the LCY Executive Bureau (later renamed Executive Committee) and retained his seat after this body was reorganized as an eight-man agency in January 1972. In October 1979 he was elected chairman of the Presidium for a one-year period. He was replaced by Lazar Mojsov of Macedonia.

DRAGOSAVAC, Dušan (Serb)

Born: 1 December 1919 in Vrebac (Croatia)
Party Membership: 1942–
Current Titles: Member of the LCY Central Committee; Secretary of the Presidium

Dragosavac was graduated from the Zagreb University Law Faculty but received his doctorate in economics in 1962. He was also graduated from the High School for Political Science in Belgrade. He joined Tito's partisans in 1941. During the war he was the political commissar of a partisan company, secretary of the Medak communal party committee, and a member of the district party committee of the Croatian party for the town of Gospić; he was later appointed secretary of the district party committee for the town of Perušić and a member of the area party committee of the same place. He was also organizational party secretary of the region of Banija and secretary of the area party committee for Karlovac. After the war Dr. Dragosavac occupied several provincial party posts until 1953 when he was appointed Croatia's minister of economics (1953–1956). From 1956 to 1958 he was Croatia's finance minister, and from 1958 to 1960 minister of trade. In 1962 he became president of the Federal Foreign Trade Chamber. He was elected a member of the Croatian Central Committee several times. At the Seventh Congress of the Croatian LC (April 1974), Dragosavac was elected secretary of the Central Committee's Executive Committee, a post he held until 1978 when, at the Eighth Congress in Zagreb, he was elected one of the three Croatian representatives on the LCY Presidium. He was reconfirmed at the Eleventh LCY Congress (1978). In May 1979 he replaced Stane Dolanc as secretary of the LCY Central Committee's Presidium.

GRLIČKOV, Aleksandar (Macedonian)

Born: 18 January 1923 in Štip (Macedonia)
Party Membership: 1943–
Current Titles: Member of the LCY Central Committee and of its Presidium (in charge of interparty relations)

Grličkov joined Tito's partisans in 1941. After the war he was graduated from the Economics Faculty of Skopje University and was chairman of the university council. He occupied various state and party posts both in Macedonia and at the federal level in Belgrade. In Macedonia he was chief of the Planning Commission, director of the Institute for Economic Planning, deputy prime minister, and prime minister. He was also a member of the Macedonian LC

Central Committee and of its Executive Committee. He was several times a member of the Macedonian National Assembly. In Belgrade Grličkov was a member of the Yugoslav Federal Assembly and deputy prime minister of Yugoslavia. At the Tenth LCY Congress (1974), he was elected to the Central Committee, the Presidium, and the Presidium's Executive Committee. Grličkov represented the LCY at all preparatory meetings for the convocation of the European communist party conferences held in Warsaw (October 1974) and Budapest (December 1974) and in East Berlin (in February, April, July, October, November, and December 1975). At the Eleventh LCY Congress (1978), Grličkov was elected a member of the Presidium as one of the three representatives of the Macedonian LC.

HERLJEVIĆ, Franjo (Croat)
Born: 21 June 1915 in Tuzla (Bosnia)
Party Membership: 1940–
Current Titles: SFRY minister of internal affairs; member of the LCY Central Committee

Colonel General Herljević joined Tito's partisan units in 1941 and occupied various military posts as company chief, battalion commander, and later brigade commander; by the end of the war he was commander of the 38th Division. After the war he was graduated from the YPA's High Military Academy and held various military posts: chief-of-staff of the YPA's Military Academy; deputy chief-of-staff of the High Military Academy; and, until 1974, secretary of national defense for the Socialist Republic of Bosnia-Herzegovina. In May 1974 Herljević was appointed Yugoslavia's minister of internal affairs, a post that he still occupies. At the Tenth (1974) and Eleventh (1978) LCY congresses, Herljević was elected a member of the Central Committee. He has the title of National Hero of Yugoslavia.

HODŽA, Fadil (Albanian)
Born: 15 March 1910 in Djakovica (Kosovo)
Party Membership: 1941–
Current Titles: Member of the State Presidency of the SFRY; member of the LCY Central Committee and of its Presidium

Before the war Hodža was an elementary school teacher. Until 1941 he lived in Albania, where he had joined "the progressive movement" in 1936 (Tito created the Albanian Communist Party only in October 1941). After returning to Yugoslavia in 1941, Hodža joined the CPY and became one of the most prominent organizers of the partisan struggle in his native town and the surrounding area. In April 1942 he was co-opted to the Bureau of the Regional Committee of the CPY for Kosovo and Metohia. In September 1942 Hodža became commander of a newly formed partisan unit, and one month later Tito appointed him chief of the military headquarters for Kosovo-Metohia. After the war he was graduated from the High School for Political Science in Belgrade and performed various duties in Kosovo: prime minister of Kosovo-Metohia (until 1963), member of the Yugoslav government (1963–1967), and then president of the National Assembly of Kosovo-Metohia. Hodža was elected a member of the central committees of the Serbian LC in January 1949 and of the LCY (since April 1958). At the Ninth LCY Congress (1969), Hodža was elected a member of the Executive Committee and retained his seat when this body was reorganized in January 1972. In May 1974 Hodža was elected Kosovo's representative on the SFRY State Presidency, and at the Tenth LCY Congress (also in May 1974) he was elected a member of the LCY Central Committee and of its Presidium, which forced him to relinquish his seat on the Executive Committee. At the Eleventh LCY Congress (1978), he was confirmed in both posts. Hodža is a National Hero of Yugoslavia.

KOLIŠEVSKI, Lazar (Macedonian)
Born: 12 February 1914 in Sveti Nikole (Macedonia)
Party Membership: 1935–
Current Titles: Member of the State Presidency of the SFRY; member of the LCY Central Committee

Before the war Koliševski was a metallurgical worker and an underground communist official in the Serbian town of Kragujevac. In 1941 after Yugoslavia's capitulation, Koliševski was sent to his native Macedonia (then occupied by the Bulgarian army) to organize the guerrilla forces and fight the Bulgarian occupation. The then secretary of the CPY Provincial Committee for Macedonia, Metodije Šatorov-Šarlo, took the Bulgarian side in the rivalry between the Yugoslav and Bulgarian communist parties and was proclaimed a traitor by Tito. After Moscow decided that the Macedonian party organization should remain within the CPY, Koliševski replaced Šatorov-Šarlo as secretary of the CPY Provincial Committee for Macedonia. Through treachery by the local Skopje branch of the party (which had transferred its allegiance to the Bulgarian Communist Party), in November 1941 Koliševski fell into the hands of the Bulgarian fascist authorities and was condemned to death. He lay in prison awaiting execution for fifteen months before his sentence was commuted to life imprisonment.

Liberated in September 1944 by the Red Army, Koliševski returned to Macedonia and in 1945 became the first prime minister of the new republic and in 1953 the president of the Macedonian National Assembly. Since 1945 he has been a member of the SFRY National Assembly. From 1953 to 1967 he was president of the Federal Committee of the SAWPY. At the Fifth LCY Congress (1948), he was elected a candidate member of the Politburo and at the Sixth (1952), Seventh (1958), and Eighth (1964) congresses was elected a member of the Presidium, a post that he occupied until April 1972 when he was elected a member of the State Presidency. At the Tenth (1974) and Eleventh (1978) LCY congresses, Koliševski was again elected a member of the Central Committee and of its Presidium. In June 1979 he was replaced in the Presidium by Lazar Mojsov. On 4 May 1980, the day of Tito's death, he was elected president of the State Presidency. But his incumbency lasted only eleven days since his one-year term as vice-president expired on 15 May 1980. Kolisevski is a National Hero of Yugoslavia.

KRAIGHER, Sergej (Slovene)
Born: 30 May 1914 in Postojna (Slovenia)
Party Membership: 1934–
Current Titles: Member of the LCY Central Committee; vice-president of the State Presidency of the SFRY

Kraigher joined Tito's partisan units in 1941 and held several party jobs, chiefly in the Slovenian party of Styria. After the war he occupied several economic posts, including that of chairman of the Slovene Republican Planning Commission (1946–1950). He was then appointed deputy prime minister of Slovenia and later governor of Yugoslavia's National Bank (1951–1953). From 1953 to 1958 Kraigher was director of the Federal Planning Institute in Belgrade, and from 1958 to 1959 SFRY minister for industry. In 1963 he was elected vice-president of the Federal Chamber and of its Committee for Socioeconomic Relations. He held these posts until his appointment as president of the National Assembly of Slovenia in 1967, in which capacity he was ex officio a member of the 23-member State Presidency established in 1971. In May 1974 Kraigher was elected to his first term as Slovenia's state president; his second term began in May 1978. In the party Kraigher first became a member of the LCY Central Committee in 1952 and later was elected to the 52-member Party Presidium set up at the Ninth LCY Congress (1969). However, he was not elected a Central Committee member either at the Tenth (1974) or Eleventh (1978) congresses. In April 1979 the Slovenian National Assembly elected him a member of the SFRY State Presidency. Several days later the Slovenian Central Committee elected him to represent Slovenia on the LCY Central Committee to replace the late Edvard Kardelj. On 15 May 1980 he was elected vice-president of the State Presidency.

LJUBIČIĆ, Nikola (Serb)
Born: 4 April 1916 in the village of Karan (Serbia)
Party Membership: 1941–
Current Titles: SFRY Secretary for National Defense; member of the LCY
Central Committee and of its Presidium

General of the Army Ljubičić was graduated before the war from the
Middle Agricultural School in Valjevo and after the war from the High Military
Academy in Belgrade. He joined Tito's partisans in 1941, when he also became a
party member. Ljubičić took part in the preparations for the armed uprising in
the district of Valjevo. During the partisan war he was successively commander of
a battalion in the Second Proletarian Brigade, an intelligence officer in a division,
commander of the Third Serbian Brigade, and chief-of-staff of the Second
Proletarian Division. After the war Ljubičić was for a time a divisional and later a
corps commander before becoming head of the School of Tactics at the High
Military Academy. In 1963 he was promoted to the rank of colonel general and in
1970 was made general of the army (the second highest military rank). Apart
from his military standing, Ljubičić is an important political figure in the party
hierarchy. At the Eighth LCY Congress (1964), Ljubičić was elected a member of
the Central Commmittee. Since May 1967 he has been state (since 1971 federal)
secretary for national defense. In 1965 he was a member of the authority
entrusted with organizing the LCY in the army.

At the Ninth LCY Congress (1969), Ljubičić was elected a member of the
Presidium and, at the Tenth LCY Congress (1974), a member of the LCY Central
Committee and of its Presidium. At the Eleventh LCY Congress (1978), he was
confirmed in these posts. General Ljubičić is a National Hero of Yugoslavia.

MAMULA, Branko (Serb)
Born: 30 May 1921 in Slavsko Polje (Croatia)
Party Membership: 1942–
Current Titles: Chief-of-staff of Yugoslavia's armed forces; member of the
LCY Central Committee

Admiral Mamula joined Tito's partisan units in 1941 and during the war
was political commissar of a battalion and a brigade. He then became political
commissar of the partisan naval units in the Croatian Maritime and Istria. By the
end of the war, he was political commissar of the Naval Headquarters for
Northern Adria. He was graduated from the High Naval Academy and attended
a military operations course at the YPA's War Academy. Following his military
studies, Admiral Mamula was appointed to a series of senior military and political
positions in the navy, among them chief-of-staff of the Navy Command and
commander of the Naval Military District, which made him ex officio the assistant
defense minister. On 15 August 1979 Tito appointed him chief-of-staff of the

Yugoslav armed forces to replace Slovene Gen. Stane Potočar. Author of a number of books, his latest is entitled *Navies on the High Seas and in Coastal Waters.* At Eleventh LCY Congress (1978), Admiral Mamula was elected a member of the LCY Central Committee to represent the party organization in the YPA. Admiral Mamula has the title of National Hero of Yugoslavia.

MARINC, Andrej (Slovene)
Born: 4 October 1930 in Celje (Slovenia)
Party Membership: 1947–
Current Titles: Deputy Prime Minister of Yugoslavia; member of the LCY Central Committee and of its Presidium

Marinc was graduated from the Faculty of Agriculture, Forestry, and Veterinary Medicine of Ljubljana University. From 1960 he worked solely in the Slovenian LC apparatus at the communal and district levels. In 1965 Marinc became a member of the Slovenian Central Committee. Only in 1978, at the Eleventh LCY Congress, was he also elected a member of the LCY Central Committee. In November 1972 he was elected Slovenia's prime minister. In May 1978 he became one of the five SFRY deputy prime ministers in Belgrade. After Kardelj's death, Marinc was elected (in June 1979) to replace him as one of the three Slovenian LC representatives on the LCY Presidium, without losing his post as SFRY deputy prime minister.

MIJATOVIĆ, Cvijetin (Serb)
Born: 8 January 1913 in the village of Popare (Bosnia)
Party Membership: 1933–
Current Titles: President of the State Presidency of the SFRY; member of the LCY Central Committee

Mijatović studied at the Philosophical Faculty of Belgrade University where he became an active party official. From 1934 to 1936 Mijatović was a member of the CPY University Committee; he was arrested several times before the war. In 1935 he was appointed instructor of the CPY Provincial Committee for Serbia and in 1938 was sent to Bosnia to set up party organizations. After his return from Bosnia, Mijatović became a member of the CPY local committee for Belgrade (1939), but in 1940 was again sent to Bosnia. He joined Tito's partisans in 1941 and organized an uprising in eastern Bosnia. In July 1941 he was appointed political commissar of partisan units in the Tuzla district and later of the Brčko partisan units, a member of the Operational Staff for Eastern Bosnia, political commissar of the Sixth East-Bosnian Proletarian Brigade, secretary of the CPY Area Committee for Eastern Bosnia, and a member of the CPY Provincial Committee for Bosnia-Herzegovina; at the second session of the AFCNLY he was elected a member of this body.

After the war Mijatović was a member of the Central Committee and organizing secretary of the Bosnian-Herzegovinian party. From 1959 to 1961 he was editorial director of the LCY's main theoretical weekly, *Komunist,* and from 1961 to 1965 he was Yugoslavia's ambassador to Moscow. From December 1964 (the Eighth LCY Congress) Mijatović became a member of the LCY Executive Committee. Since October 1966 he has been a member of the Presidium. From 1965 to 1969 Mijatović was at first secretary and later president of the Central Committee of the Bosnian-Herzegovinian LC. In March 1969 he was removed from that position and in January 1972 relinquished his seat on the Executive Bureau when it was reorganized as an eight-man body. At the Tenth (1974) and Eleventh (1978) LCY congresses, Mijatović was elected to the Central Committee and to its Presidium. In June 1979, however, he was replaced in the Presidium by the Moslem Hamdija Pozderac. On 15 May 1980 he was elected president of the State Presidency for a one-year period. Mijatović is a National Hero of Yugoslavia.

MIKULIĆ, Branko (Croat)
Born: 10 June 1928 in the village of Podgradje (Bosnia-Herzegovina)
Party Membership: 1945–
Current Titles: Member of the LCY Central Committee and of its Presidium

At fifteen, Mikulić joined Tito's partisans but held no important post. After the war he was graduated from the Zagreb Economic High School. He was secretary of the Youth Federation of Yugoslavia in Gornji Vakuf and Bugojno, organizational secretary of the district party committees in Bugojno and Jajce, secretary of the district party committees in Livno and Zenica, and in 1965 was elected a member of the Bosnian-Herzegovinian Central Committee and secretary of its Executive Committee. In 1967 Mikulić became prime minister of Bosnia-Herzegovina, holding this post until his appointment in 1969 as president of the Bosnian-Herzegovinian Central Committee. He was confirmed in office by the Sixth Congress of the Bosnian-Herzegovinian LC (March 1974). At the Tenth (1974) and Eleventh (1978) LCY congresses, Mikulić was elected a member of the Central Committee and of its Presidium (in 1974 ex officio and in 1978 directly). In October 1978 Mikulić was elected chairman of the Presidium for a one-year period and was replaced in October 1979 by Stevan Doronjski.

MINIĆ, Miloš (Serb)
Born: 28 August 1914 in the village of Preljina (Serbia)
Party Membership: 1936–
Current Titles: Member of the LCY Central Committee and of its Presidium

Minić was graduated from the Law Faculty of Belgrade University in 1938 and practiced law before the war. He was also a prominent member of the communist youth movement. While a student, Minić was first a member of the faculty CPY committee and later of the university party committee. In 1939 he was a member of the CPY district committee in Čačak. From May 1940 to March 1941 Minić went underground and as an instructor of the Serbian Provincial Committee of the CPY tried to renew the party organization in the Serbian town of Kruševac. He joined Tito's partisans in 1941 and was one of the organizers of the armed struggle in western Serbia, where he worked as an instructor of the provincial committee in the Valjevo district. In 1943 and 1944 Minić was secretary of the CPY district committee in Čačak. After the war Minić was appointed chief of the secret police and state prosecutor in Serbia. Minić was chief prosecutor at the trial of the anticommunist guerrilla leader Gen. Dragoljub-Draža Mihailović, who was sentenced to death and executed in July 1946.

Between 1950 and 1957 Minić performed various duties as a Serbian and federal minister and in 1957 was appointed prime minister of Serbia (1957–1962). From 1963 to 1966 Minić was deputy prime minister of Yugoslavia in charge of planning. In 1966 and 1967 he was chairman of the Federal Chamber of Yugoslavia's Federal Assembly, then president of Serbia's National Assembly (1967–1969). In 1969 he was elected a member of the Chamber of Nationalities and became vice-president of the Federal Assembly. In December 1972 he was appointed Yugoslavia's deputy prime minister and foreign minister after his predecessor Mirko Tepavac was purged for "liberalist deviations."

In the LCY Minić was elected a candidate member of the Central Committee in 1948. At the next three congresses he was elected a full member of the Central Committee. At the Ninth LCY Congress (1969), Minić was not elected to the Presidium, but at the Tenth (1974) and Eleventh (1978) congresses he was elected a member of both the LCY Central Committee and of its Presidium. Minić is a National Hero of Yugoslavia.

MOJSOV, Lazar (Macedonian)
Born: 19 December 1920 in Negotino (Macedonia)
Party Membership: 1940–
Current Titles: Member of the LCY Central Committee; President of the Presidium

Mojsov joined Tito's partisan units in 1941 and occupied various political posts within the Macedonian partisan headquarters. After the war he was graduated from the Law Faculty of Belgrade University and assumed various duties in the Macedonian government in Skopje, among them chief public prosecutor and director of the newspaper *Nova Makedonija.* At the federal level, Mojsov joined the diplomatic service and was Yugoslavia's ambassador to the Soviet Union (1958–1961), Austria (1967–1969), and the United Nations (1969–1974), where he was twice elected president of the U.N. Security Council. Afterward, he became Yugoslavia's deputy foreign minister and in that capacity was elected (in June 1977) president of the U.N. General Assembly. In Yugoslavia his other jobs were director of the Institute for the Workers' Movement and editor-in-chief of *Borba*. At the Seventh (1958) and Eighth (1964) LCY congresses, Mojsov was elected a member of the Central Committee. At the Ninth Congress (1969), when a Presidium instead of a Central Committee was created, Mojsov was not elected, but at the Tenth (1974) and Eleventh (1978) congresses, he was again elected a Central Committee member. In June 1979 Mojsov replaced Lazar Koliševski as Macedonian representative on the Presidium.

PLANINC, Milka (Croat)
Born: 21 November 1924 in Drniš (Croatia)
Party Membership: 1944–
Current Titles: President of the Central Committee of the Croatian LC; ex officio member both of the LCY Central Committee and of its Presidium

Mme. Planinc was graduated from the Higher Administration School in Zagreb. She joined Tito's partisans in 1941. After the war she pursued a full-time political career in the Croatian LC, specializing in agitprop and education. In 1954 she became a party instructor in the Zagreb Municipal Party Committee, was later political secretary of the Trešnjevka (Zagreb) Municipal Party Committee, and in 1957 president of the Trešnjevka People's Committee. After serving as the head of the Zagreb People's Committee Secretariat for Education and Culture, she became (in 1963) the organizational secretary of the Zagreb Municipal Party Committee and (in 1965) the republican secretary of education. In 1966 she was elected to the Presidium of the Croatian LC and in 1968 to its Executive Committee.

Planinc's real party career began in December 1971 after Tito purged the top Croatian party and state leaders and she was elected president of the Central Committee of the Croatian LC and helped Tito suppress Croatian nationalism. She was confirmed in her offices both at the Seventh Congress of the Croatian LC (April 1974) and at the Tenth (1974) and Eleventh (1978) LCY congresses.

POPIT, Franc (Slovene)
Born: 3 August 1921 in Vrhnika (Slovenia)
Party Membership: 1940–
Current Titles: President of the Central Committee of the Slovenian LC; ex officio member both of the LCY Central Committee and of its Presidium

Little is known about Popit's early life; he seems to have been a professional party apparatchik, especially in the Youth Federation of Yugoslavia, which he joined in 1936. He joined Tito's partisans in 1941 and was secretary of a district party committee,. an instructor for CPY organizations in Slovenia, and political commissar of the Slovenian operational zone. From 1944 to 1945 he held various senior posts in the Slovenian political-military administration. After the war Popit was secretary general of the office of the prime minister of Slovenia, forestry minister in the Slovenian government, secretary of labor in the federal government, secretary of the Slovenian LC in Kranj and Ljubljana, president of the Trade Union Federation of Slovenia, a member of the Central Council of the Yugoslav Trade Union Confederation, and secretary of the Executive Committee of the Slovenian Central Committee. At all congresses of the Slovenian LC, he was elected to the Central Committee. At the Eighth LCY Congress (1964), he was elected a member of the LCY Central Committee. At the Ninth LCY Congress (1969), he was elected a member of the Presidium. At the Seventh Congress of the Slovenian LC (April 1974), he was re-elected to his post. At the Tenth (1974) and Eleventh (1978) LCY congresses (June 1978), he was confirmed in his posts.

POZDERAC, Hamdija (Moslem)
Born: 15 December 1923 in Cazin (Bosnia)
Party Membership: 1943–
Current Titles: Member of the LCY Central Committee and of its Presidium

Pozderac joined Tito's partisan units in 1942. He was graduated from the Philosophical Faculty and High Party School in Moscow. Both during and after his education, he occupied local party posts. In 1965 he was elected a member of the Central Committee of Bosnian-Herzegovinian LC and a member of its Executive Committee. At the Eleventh LCY Congress (1978), Pozderac was elected a member of the LCY Central Committee. At the sixth plenary session of the Central Committee in June 1979, he was elected to replace Cvijetin Mijatović (a Serb) as one of the three representatives of the Bosnian-Herzegovinian LC on the LCY Presidium.

SRZENTIĆ, Vojo (Montenegrin)
Born: 31 November 1934 in Sotonići (Montenegro)
Party Membership: 1952–
Current Titles: President of the Montenegrin LC Central Committee; ex officio member of the LCY Central Committee and of its Presidium

Srzentić was a child during the war and only after it became involved in governmental and party activities in Montenegro. He was graduated from the

Economics Faculty of Belgrade University in 1954. In 1958 he was made secretary of the communal assembly in the town of Bar. Later he became president of the Montenegrin party youth organization. At the Fourth (March 1965), Fifth (December 1968), and Sixth (April 1974) congresses of the Montenegrin LC, Srzentić was elected a member of the Montenegrin Central Committee and of its Executive Committee, whose secretary he later became. After Veselin Djuranović was appointed prime minister of Yugoslavia in March 1977, Srzentić became president of the Central Committee of the Montenegrin LC and as such ex officio a member of the LCY Presidium. At the Tenth LCY Congress (1974), Srzentić was elected a member of the Central Committee and a secretary of the Presidium's Executive Committee (abolished at the Eleventh LCY Congress in 1978). At the Seventh Congress of the Montenegrin LC (April 1978), Srzentić was confirmed in his position as president of the Montenegrin Central Committee.

STAMBOLIĆ, Petar (Serb)

Born: 12 May 1912 in the village of Brezova (Serbia)
Party Membership: 1935–
Current Titles: Member of the State Presidency of the SFRY; member of the
LCY Central Committee and of its Presidium

Stambolić was graduated from the Agricultural Faculty of Belgrade University. Before the war he was arrested many times because of his communist underground activities. In 1941 Stambolić joined Tito's partisans and was one of the organizers of resistance in Serbia. He himself led the underground movement in Belgrade and in 1944 became commander-in-chief of the Serbian partisan units. From 1945 to 1948 Stambolić held senior posts in the Serbian and federal governments and between 1948 and 1953 was prime minister of Serbia. He was successively president of the Serbian National Assembly (1953–1957), president of the Yugoslav National Assembly (1957–1963), and Yugoslavia's prime minister (1963–1967). Since 1945 he has been a member of the Yugoslav National Assembly. Stambolić was secretary of the Serbian LC Central Committee (1948–1957), a member of the LCY Central Committee (later Presidium), and between 1954 and 1966 a member of the party's Executive Committee. From 1966 to 1969 Stambolić was president of the Serbian LC Central Committee. Since he relinquished the prime ministership of Yugoslavia in 1967, he has been less prominent but was elected to the LCY Presidium at the Ninth (1969), Tenth (1974), and Eleventh (1978) congresses. Although he has occupied many top state and party positions both in Serbia and Yugoslavia, he cannot be considered

Serbia's number-one man. He has always belonged to that group of Serbian communist leaders inclined toward a strong-arm regime. Stambolić is a National Hero of Yugoslavia.

STOJANOVIĆ, Nikola (Serb)
Born: 19 August 1933 in Ljubija (Bosnia)
Party Membership: 1952–
Current Titles: President of the Central Committee of the Bosnian-Herzego-
vinian LC; ex officio member both of the LCY Central
Committee and of its Presidium

Stojanović was too young to join Tito's partisans during the war. An economist, he began his career in Bosnia-Herzegovina in the Planning Institution in Sarajevo. He was also a lecturer at the High School for Political Science in Belgrade. At the Sixth Congress of the Bosnian-Herzegovinian LC (March 1974), Stojanović was elected secretary of the Central Committee's Executive Committee. At the Seventh Congress (May 1978), he was elected president of the Bosnian-Herzegovinian Central Committee, which made him ex officio a member of the LCY Central Committee and of its Presidium.

VLAŠKALIĆ, Dr. Tihomir (Serb)
Born: 1 January 1923 in Kula (Vojvodina)
Party Membership: 1945–
Current Titles: President of the Central Committee of the Serbian LC; ex
officio member of the LCY Central Committee and of its
Presidium

Dr. Vlaškalić was graduated from the Economics Faculty of Belgrade University in 1949 and in 1950 became a lecturer there. In 1957 he acquired his doctorate with a dissertation entitled "Agrarian Reform in the SFRY, 1945." In 1962 Vlaškalić became an associate professor and in 1968 a full professor of the Economics Faculty. He joined Tito's partisans in 1944. After the war Vlaškalić wrote several studies on the Yugoslav economy. Both in the Serbian National Assembly and in the Central Committee of the Serbian LC, Vlaškalić played a role as a prominent economist. In 1959 he was sent to England for specialized training and in 1960–1961 was a member of the U.N. Economic Commission in Geneva. Dr. Vlaškalić's party career started in November 1972 when he was elected president of the Serbian Central Committee after his predecessor, Marko Nikezić, had been purged by Tito as an "anarcho-liberal." He was re-elected at the Seventh Congress of the Serbian LC (April 1974). At the Tenth (1974) and Eleventh (1978) LCY congresses, he was confirmed in his posts.

ŽARKOVIĆ, Vidoje (Montenegrin)
Born: 10 June 1927 in Piva (Montenegro)
Party Membership: 1943–
Current Title: Member of the State Presidency of the SFRY

Žarković was graduated from the High Military Naval Academy and from the High School for Political Science in Belgrade. He joined Tito's partisans in 1941. After the war he was a member of the Political Administration of the Yugoslav Navy, director of the Institution of Electronics, and head of the Department of the Yugoslav Navy. He also played an important role in the People's Youth of Yugoslavia and Montenegro. From 1966 to 1968 Žarković was secretary of the Central Committee of the Montenegrin LC. He was a member of its Presidium until May 1967, when he was appointed prime minister of Montenegro. Between 1969 and 1972 he was president of the Montenegrin National Assembly. As a member of the LCY Presidium in 1969, he sat on the Commission for Economic Policy. In 1971 his membership as representative of Montenegro in the State Presidency of the SFRY (at that time composed of 23 members) was confirmed; he was re-elected in 1974 to the same post (now an eight-man body). At the Tenth (1974) and Eleventh (1978) LCY congresses, Žarković was confirmed in his posts. In June 1979, however, he was replaced on the Presidium by Dobroslav Ćulafić.

Notes

CHAPTER ONE

1. Yugoslavia is composed of six socialist republics (Slovenia, Croatia, Bosnia-Herzegovina, Montenegro, Macedonia, and Serbia) and (within the Socialist Republic of Serbia) two autonomous provinces (Vojvodina and Kosovo). Each republic and autonomous province has its own three-chamber assembly (Chamber of Associated Labor, Chamber of Communes, and Sociopolitical Chamber). In addition, each republic and autonomous province has its own Executive Council (government).

   At the federal level the Assembly of the SFRY is composed of two chambers: the Federal Chamber with 220 delegates (30 delegates from each of the six republics and 20 delegates from each of the two autonomous provinces) elected by communal assemblies in secret ballots on the basis of a list of candidates; the Chamber of Republics and Autonomous Provinces with 88 delegates (12 from each of the six republics and 8 from each of the two autonomous provinces) elected by republican and provincial assemblies.

   The executive body of the Assembly of the SFRY is the Federal Executive Council (the government), consisting of a president (prime minister) and five vice-presidents (deputy prime ministers) and 23 other members.

   The supreme ruling body, however, is the Presidency of the SFRY (popularly known as the State Presidency), composed of eight members (one from each of the six republics and two autonomous provinces) elected for a five-year term and—as of February 1980—seven ex officio members: the president of the Assembly of the SFRY, Yugoslavia's prime minister, the chairman of the LCY Central Committee Presidium, the secretary of the Presidium, the defense minister, the interior minister, and the foreign minister.

   With Tito's death, the post of president of the Republic no longer exists; instead, the State Presidency now acts as a collective state leadership and, according to the constitution (Article 319), appears to have more power than the Assembly of the SFRY, in the case of a conflict between the two bodies.

2. Vladimir Goati, "Društveno-političke organizacije i samoupravni interes" [Sociopolitical organizations and self-management interests], *Gledišta* 1978, no. 4 (April): 305.

3. *Vjesnik*, 19 May 1979.
4. *Borba*, 24 December 1953.
5. Edvard Kardelj, *Pravci razvoja političkog sistema socijalističkog samoupravljanja* [Roads of development of the socialist self-management political system], 2nd rev. ed. (Belgrade: Publishing House Komunist, 1978), p. 204.
6. *Borba*, 8 May 1979.
7. Ibid.
8. Andrija Krešić, "Principi rukovodjenja u Savezu komunista" [Principles of management in the League of Communists], *Gledišta* 1967, no. 1 (January): 34.

CHAPTER TWO

1. The nationality problem has plagued Yugoslavia ever since its foundation in December 1918, when it was called the Kingdom of the Serbs, Croats, and Slovenes. This name was changed in January 1929 to the Kingdom of Yugoslavia, i.e., the kingdom of the Southern Slavs. From 1918 to 1941, when Hitler and his allies destroyed Yugoslavia, only three "tribes" were recognized: the Serbs, Croats, and Slovenes, who, it was claimed officially, were a single nation with three names. All the other nationalities of Slav origin (notably the Macedonians and Montenegrins) were attached to one of these three "tribes," all, however, belonging to a united "Yugoslav nation." According to the March 1971 census there are eighteen ethnic minority groups in Yugoslavia (officially called "nationalities" to distinguish them from the six "leading nations"). Before the last war they did not enjoy any special privileges (especially the Albanians), and it was therefore easy for the "mother countries" bordering Yugoslavia to incite them against the Yugoslav state. They constitute approximately 10 percent of Yugoslavia's current population of 22 million. According to the March 1971 census (*Yugoslav Survey*, Belgrade, no. 1 [February 1973]), six leading nations (in place of the former three tribes) are recognized: the Serbs (8,143,932), the Croats (4,526,782), the Slav Moslems (1,729,932), the Slovenes (1,678,032), the Macedonians (1,194,784), and the Montenegrins (508,843). Except for the Slovenes, who live in a compact national group, the other nationalities have become deeply intermixed (especially the Serbs and the Croats), with the result that their mutual relations have suffered severely from national animosities. Before 1918 they lived either as separate nations in their own states (the Serbs and Montenegrins) or were parts of other states (for instance of the Austro-Hungarian monarchy and of Turkey). Their different traditions, backgrounds, and religions made it very difficult for them to abandon all this overnight and become one nation.
2. *Politika*, 8 June 1968.
3. *Ekonomska politika*, 18 September 1978.

4. *Vjesnik*, 11 October 1978.
5. Ibid.
6. Ibid.
7. *Politika*, 28 September 1978.
8. *Večernje novosti*, 5 October 1978.
9. Ibid.
10. *Dnevnik* (Ljubljana), 15 October 1979.
11. *Socialist Thought and Practice* (Belgrade), 1979, no. 10 (October): 50. According to the *Journal of Commerce* (New York) [25 September 1979], Yugoslavia's foreign debts are estimated at between $11 and $13 billion.
12. *Borba*, 21 September 1979.
13. *Vjesnik*, 13 August 1979.
14. Ibid., 8 August 1979.
15. *NIN*, 15 October 1978.
16. *Večernje novosti*, 21 September 1978.
17. *Ekonomska politika*, 7 August 1978.
18. *NIN*, 15 October 1978.
19. Ibid.
20. Ibid.
21. *Ekonomska politika*, 10 September 1979.
22. At a symposium held in Belgrade on 10 December 1971 under the title "Kako je socijalizam danas moguć?" [How Is Socialism Today Possible?], *Gledišta* 1972, no. 2 (February): 234–35.
23. *Encounter* no. 2 (February) 1979.
24. *Gledišta* 1978, no. 6 (June): 527.
25. Ibid.
26. Ibid.
27. Ibid.
28. Žarko Papić, "The Socialist Market Economy and Economic Development," *Socialist Thought and Practice* 1978, no. 11/12 (November/December): 53.
29. James Burnham, *The Managerial Revolution* (New York: John Day, 1941), pp. 92–93.
30. Ibid., p. 123.
31. Žarko Ilić, "Alternativni pristupi ekonomskim konfliktima" [Alternative approaches to the economic conflicts], *Gledišta* 1978, no. 6 (June): 534.
32. Miladin Korać, *Socijalistički samoupravni način proizvodnje* [The socialist self-management way of production] (Belgrade: Komunist Publishing House, 1977), p. 20.
33. Ilić, "Alternativni pristupi."
34. *Die Welt* (Bonn), 28 October 1978.

35. *The Programme of the League of Yugoslav Communists* (Belgrade: Edition Jugoslavija, 1958), p. 270.
36. *Politika*, 21 April 1964.
37. *Vjesnik*, 27 August 1978.
38. Ibid., 2 September 1978.
39. Ibid.
40. Ibid.
41. *Start*, 6 September 1978.
42. *NIN*, 20 August 1978.
43. *Naše teme*, 1978, no. 1 (January): 100.
44. Ibid., p. 99.

CHAPTER THREE

1. *Programme of the LCY*, p. 270.
2. *Programme of the Communist Party of the Soviet Union* (Moscow: Foreign Languages Publishing House, 1961), pp. 20, 41.
3. *NIN*, 9 October 1977.
4. Ibid.
5. Ibid.
6. *Komunist*, 6 February 1978.
7. *Vjesnik*, 6 April 1979.
8. *Borba*, 20 April 1979.
9. Ibid.
10. The interview with Dr. Bakarić appeared in the West German daily *Die Welt*, 20 June 1978, but without the statement about pluralism in the West mentioned in the text. This was published in the Serbo-Croat version of the interview in *Vjesnik*, 1 July 1978, and in *NIN*, 9 July 1978.
11. *Vjesnik*, 6 April 1978.

CHAPTER FOUR

1. *The Military Balance, 1979–80* (London: International Institute for Strategic Studies, 1979), p. 35.
2. *Borba*, 24 December 1971.
3. Ibid., 23 December 1971.
4. Ibid., 24 December 1971.
5. *Vjesnik*, 18 March 1971.

6. *Frankfurter Rundschau*, 17 December 1971.
7. *Hrvatski tjednik*, 5 November 1971.
8. *Službeni list* [Official gazette] (Belgrade), 4 May 1974, p. 647.
9. *Borba*, 6 June 1970.
10. *Front*, 3 May 1974.
11. *Vojno delo* 1970, no. 2 (March/April): 86—99.
12. *Vjesnik*, 21 April 1979.
13. Ibid.
14. *Svenarodna obrana*, August/September 1972, pp. 27—31.
15. *Vjesnik*, 11 January 1971.
16. *Socialist Thought and Practice* 1974, no. 4 (April): 103.
17. *Službeni list*, 4 May 1974, p. 646.
18. Ibid., p. 647.
19. *Socialist Thought and Practice* 1974, no. 4 (April): 103.
20. Ibid., p. 104.
21. Ibid.
22. Ibid., p. 105.
23. *Službeni list*, 4 May 1974, p. 649.
24. Sveto Kovačević, *Odjek* no. 13/14 (July 1970): 12.
25. General Dusăn Dozet, "Društveni činioci opštenarodne odbrane" [Social factors of the nationwide defense system], Part 1, *Narodna Armija*, 19 June 1970.
26. *Komunist*, 18 June 1970; see especially the report by Gen. Božo Šašić, "Položaj pojedinca u armiji samoupravnog društva" [The Position of the individual in the army of the self-management society].
27. Tanjug, 5 April 1979.
28. Ibid.
29. *Borba*, 27 December 1978.
30. Ibid.
31. *Narodna armija*, 31 August 1978.
32. *Review of International Affairs* no. 656/657 (5—20 August 1977).
33. A. Ross Johnson, *The Role of the Military in Communist Yugoslavia: A Historical Sketch* (Santa Monica, Calif.: Rand Corp., 1978), p. 16. (The data for the Eleventh LCY Congress are from Slobodan Stanković).
34. *Komunist*, 30 June 1978.
35. *Odjek* no. 13/14 (July 1970).
36. *Politika*, 23 May 1970.
37. *Socijalizam*, 1973, no. 1 (January).
38. Ibid.
39. *Österreichische Militärische Zeitschrift* (Vienna), March/April 1971.

40. Jovan Djordjević, *Politički sistem: Prilog nauci o čoveku i samoupravljanju* [The political system: A contribution to the science of man and self-management] (Belgrade: Privredni Pregled, 1973), p. 606.

41. *Večernje novosti*, 16 August 1979.

42. *Narodna armija*, 16 May 1980.

43. *Službeni list*, 4 May 1974, pp. 647−48.

44. *Narodna armija*, 16 May 1980.

45. *Službeni list*, 4 May 1974, p. 648.

CHAPTER FIVE

1. *Frankfurter Allgemeine Zeitung*, 15 February 1967.

2. *Oslobodjenje*, 2 December 1968.

3. *Službeni list*, 15 February 1980.

4. *Vjesnik*, 23 September 1970.

5. *Službeni list*, 8 July 1971.

6. *Borba*, 3 February 1979.

7. Tanjug, 5 February 1979.

8. *Službeni list*, 7 March 1975.

9. *Borba*, 22 November 1978.

10. Ibid.

11. Ibid., 5 January 1979.

12. Ibid., 9 December 1978.

13. Ibid., 8 December 1978.

14. Ibid., 7 January 1979.

15. Ibid.

16. Ibid.

17. Ibid., 5 January 1979.

18. *Politika*, 29 June 1979.

19. *Komunist*, 27 March 1978, special supplement.

20. *Vjesnik*, 15 July 1979.

21. Milovan Djilas, *The Unperfect Society: Beyond the New Class* (New York: Harcourt Brace & World, 1969), p. 194.

22. Milovan Djilas, *Wartime* (New York: Harcourt Brace Jovanovich, 1977), p. 344.

23. *The Soviet-Yugoslav Dispute* (London: Royal Institute of International Affairs, 1948).

24. *Vjesnik*, 16 May 1979.

25. *Komunist*, 27 March 1978, special supplement.

26. Ibid.
27. *Komunist*, 18 May 1979.
28. Dusko Doder, *The Yugoslavs* (New York: Random House, 1978), p. 74.
29. *Komunist*, 10 November 1978, special supplement.
30. *NIN*, 26 November 1978.
31. *Komunist*, 10 November 1978, special supplement.
32. Ibid.
33. *NIN*, 26 November 1978.
34. *Komunist*, 10 November 1978, special supplement.
35. *NIN*, 26 November 1978.
36. *Borba*, 24 October 1979.
37. *Politika*, 19 October 1979.
38. *Borba*, 24 July 1979.
39. *Komunist*, 1 June 1979.
40. *Politika*, 19 October 1979.
41. *Vjesnik*, 13 June 1976.

CHAPTER SIX

1. *Politika*, 24 September 1971.
2. *Vjesnik*, 23 February 1973.
3. *Politika*, 2 November 1972.
4. *Vjesnik*, 16 September 1972.
5. Ibid., 24 May 1973.
6. Ibid.
7. *Borba*, 22 May 1979.
8. *Pravda* (Moscow), 20 May 1979.
9. Tass, 21 May 1979.
10. *Vjesnik*, 24 October 1976.
11. Ibid., 21 July 1979.
12. Zorica Priklmajer-Tomanović, *Evrokomunizam* [Eurcommunism] (Belgrade: NIP Politika, 1978).
13. Kardelj, *Pravci razvoja*, p. 47.
14. Ibid., p. 52.
15. Ibid., p. 50.
16. Vladimir Dedijer, *Tito Speaks* (London: Weidenfeld & Nicolson, 1953), p. 304.
17. *Komunist*, 6 July 1979.
18. *Politika*, 4 July 1979.

19. *Vjesnik*, 27 June 1979.

20. André Harris and Alain Sedony, *Voyage à l'intérieur du parti communiste* (Paris: Seuil, 1974), pp. 429–30. (*Politika* [29 September 1979] attacked Marchais for his approval of the Vietnamese invasion of Cambodia.)

21. *NIN*, 10 June 1979.

22. Santiago Carrillo, *"Eurocommunism" and the State* (London: Lawrence & Wishart, 1977).

23. *Vjesnik*, 11 October 1969.

24. For the origins and process of the Tito-Stalin conflict of 1948, see Adam B. Ulam, *Titoism and the Cominform* (Cambridge, Mass.: Harvard University Press, 1952); see also Vladimir Dedijer, *Tito Speaks: His Self Portrait and Struggle With Stalin* (London: Weidenfeld & Nicolson, 1953). For the 1955 reconciliation between Belgrade and Moscow, see Chapter 20 (pp. 417–54), "Foreign Policy: East? West? or Both?" in George W. Hoffman and Fred Warren Neal, *Yugoslavia and the New Communism* (New York: Twentieth Century Fund, 1952).

25. *Borba*, 30 June 1948.

26. Ibid., 20 June 1978.

27. Predrag Vranicki, *Marksizam i socijalizam* (Zagreb: Liber, 1979).

28. *Pravda*, 13 July 1979.

29. *NIN*, 12 August 1979.

30. *Komunist*, 17 August 1979.

31. *Večernji list*, 30 August 1979.

32. *Review of International Affairs* no. 652, 20 June 1977.

33. Ibid.

34. Ibid.

35. *Vjesnik*, 16 July 1979.

36. *Komunist*, 4 May 1979.

37. *Vjesnik*, 8 September 1979.

38. *Borba*, 11 September 1979.

39. *Politika*, 5 September 1979.

40. Ibid.

41. Radio Ljubljana, 6 September 1979.

42. *Borba*, 24 September 1979.

43. *Politika*, 24 September 1979.

44. Ibid.

45. *Vjesnik*, 28 September 1979.

46. Ibid.

47. Milovan Djilas, "Yugoslavia in Danger," *Encounter* 1979, no. 9 (September): 65.

48. Ibid.

49. *Hrvatska država* (Munich), February/March 1971.

50. *Danica* (Chicago), no. 11, 14 March 1960.
51. *Hrvatski list* (Lund, Sweden), no. 3, 1 March 1980.
52. *NIN*, 29 July 1979. (*Borba* [15 October 1979] said that "about 1,500,000 inhabitants now live in a territory of 10,800 sq. km.)
53. *Borba*, 22 March 1979.
54. *Pravda*, 1 June 1980.
55. *Večernji list*, 2 June 1980.
56. *NIN*, 1 June 1980.
57. *Komunist*, 30 May 1980.

CHAPTER SEVEN

1. *NIN*, 28 October 1979.
2. Ibid.
3. *Borba*, 19 October 1979.
4. After Ćulafić was elected a member of the Presidium on 28 June 1979, he was replaced as president of the Federal Chamber by Mme. Stana Tomašević-Arnesen (also from Montenegro), the former Yugoslav ambassador to Denmark.
5. *NIN*, 28 October 1979.
6. *Arhiv za pravne i društvene nauke* [Archives for legal and social sciences] (Belgrade), 1962, no. 3/4 (March/April): 346.
7. *NIN*, 28 October 1979.
8. Djordjević, *Politički sistem*, p. 776.
9. *Politika*, 24 October 1979.
10. Mihajlo Mihajlov, "The Dissident Movement in Yugoslavia," *Washington Quarterly* 1979 (Autumn).
11. *Borba*, 6 July 1976; and *Vjesnik*, 15 April 1978.
12. *Politika*, 8 June 1978.
13. *Večernje novosti*, 19 January 1974.
14. *Komunist*, 25 February 1974.
15. *Süddeutsche Zeitung*, 8 July 1974.
16. *Die Welt*, 27 October 1979.
17. *Life Magazine*, 1 May 1970, p. 64.
18. *Politika*, 16 October 1979.
19. Ibid.
20. *Borba*, 22 October 1979.
21. For the Serbian Central Committee plenum, see *Politika*, 14 March 1980; for the Croatian Central Committee plenum, *Vjesnik*, 19 March 1980.
22. *Politika*, 21 May 1980.

23. Ibid.
24. *Vjesnik*, 23 May 1980.
25. *Večernje novosti*, 22 May 1980.
26. *Vjesnik*, 22 May 1980.
27. *Večernje novosti*, 22 May 1980.
28. *Vjesnik*, 23 May 1980.
29. *Borba*, 22 May 1980.
30. *Vecernje novosti*, 22 May 1980. (The Zagreb daily *Vjesnik* of 22 May 1980 claimed that this suggestion implied that the prime minister would be immediately elected for a four-year term).
31. *Borba*, 22 May 1980; *Večernji list*, 31 July 1980.
32. *Ustav Socijalisticke Federativne Republike Jugoslavije* [Constitution of the Socialist Federative Republic of Yugoslavia] (Belgrade: Službeni list, 1974): 162–63.
33. *NIN*, 25 May 1980.
34. *Službeni list*, 7 March 1975.
35. *Borba*, 13 and 14 June 1980.

APPENDIX

1. In its 10 May issue, the Zagreb daily *Vjesnik* confirmed long-standing claims that President Tito was born on 7 May 1892 rather than on 25 May, the officially celebrated day. According to the paper, the date 7 May is to be found in the birth registry of the Catholic parish of Tuhelj, under whose jurisdiction Tito's birthplace, Kumrovec, fell at the time of his birth. The paper also said that "in some of the Broz family's documents his birthday is given differently." For this reason, during the last war "some of Tito's colleagues began celebrating 25 May as his birthday," a practice that was continued "after the liberation, and that since 1957 has also been celebrated as the Day of Youth."

2. Walter Roberts, *Tito, Mihailovich and the Allies, 1941–1945* (New Brunswick, N.J.: Rutgers University Press, 1973), p. 108.

Index